THE
LEADERSHIP
ROUTE

THE LEADERSHIP ROUTE

HOW DIFFERENT APPROACHES TO MANAGEMENT CAN SHAPE A LEADER

ALEX CUMMINS

WILEY

This edition first published 2025.
© 2025 by John Wiley & Sons Ltd.

The right of Alex Cummins to be identified as the author of this work has been asserted in accordance with law.

Registered Offices
John Wiley & Sons, Inc., 111 River Street, Hoboken, NJ 07030, USA
John Wiley & Sons Ltd, The Atrium, Southern Gate, Chichester, West Sussex, PO19 8SQ, UK

For details of our global editorial offices, customer services, and more information about Wiley products visit us at www.wiley.com.

Wiley also publishes its books in a variety of electronic formats and by print-on-demand. Some content that appears in standard print versions of this book may not be available in other formats.

Library of Congress Cataloging-in-Publication Data is Available:

ISBN 9781394325238 (Cloth)
ISBN 9781394325450 (ePub)
ISBN 9781394325467 (ePDF)

Cover Design: Wiley
Cover Image: © MicroStockHub/Getty Images
Author Photo: Courtesy of Alex Cummins

Set in 12/21 pts D-DIN Condensed by Straive, Chennai, India

SKY10097566_013025

FOR MUM AND DAD, WHO NEVER STOPPED BELIEVING IN ME.

CONTENTS

About the Author

Alex Cummins was born in 1980 in Essex to a Malaysian mother and a Scottish father. From an early age, he was excited by this cross-cultural identity and developed a fascination for language and culture. He went on to study a Major in Thai literature at the University of London. After graduating, Alex realised that his passion was learning about people and helping them succeed.

His journey in education has led him all over Asia, culminating in the founding of Mango Training and Consultancy in Malaysia in 2011.

Alex has trained and coached managers and leaders from many different industries including banking and finance to government-linked organisations all over the world. *The Leadership Route* draws on hundreds of hours of coaching, training and informal discussions with people from all sectors and levels in some of the biggest global organisations.

Acknowledgments

There are many people who I would like to thank for the conversations, debates and downloads that helped me put this book together. First, thank you to my team at Mango who have helped lift others all over the world and continue to do so. A huge thanks to all the clients who believed and continue to believe in Mango. Thank you to the inspirational leaders whose conversations have helped me grow, like Datuk Kelvin Tan, Eric Lee, Charles Bhatana and Baskaran Batamalai. Thank you to Neil Sandilands who showed me the power of reinvention and a growth mindset as well as true friendship. A massive thanks to Toby Merlot who picked me up when I was down. Finally, a huge thank you to my wife and son who let me work when I should have been playing.

Introducing Mango Bank

Mango Bank Tower stands in the heart of Singapore's financial district, its 58 floors paying tribute to the organisation's global business success and stability. The Bank is famous for its bright orange logo and quirky branding that have made it synonymous with modernity and tech savviness. Behind the scenes, Mango Bank is going through periods of immense change. Restructuring and automation have helped cultivate not only a sense of excitement but also trepidation about the bank's future.

Mango Bank's footprints stretch far beyond Singapore and its offices from Oslo to Osaka work through a vast interconnected network to supply financial services across the world. Headquartered in Singapore, Mango Bank Tower is where the strategic direction for the bank is set and on its 58th floor, its enigmatic CEO Rupert Wong, endlessly squeezed by his shareholders, looks out into the Singapore horizon. His serene expression belies the uncertainty he feels as Mango Bank stands at the crossroads of tradition and modernity.

Below him, the office is abuzz with activity. Powerful executives in tailored suits rub shoulders with younger tech whizz kids in smart casual attire. Conversations are a mixture of financial jargon and speculation about the Bank's next big move. On one floor, a group of IT managers gather around a huge screen discussing an AI interphase that promises to bring the Bank even closer to its customers. On another floor, senior leaders are plotting a complex matrix of nodes and links that resemble a drunken spider's web across a training room's vinyl walls. Meanwhile, further down, operational employees sit quietly, intently focused on checking documents punctuated only by the occasional sip of dark coffee.

The walls of Mango Bank are adorned with bright posters sharing the Bank's values and championing the behaviours of risk-taking and customer centricity. Staff wear bright lanyards that profess the Mango Bank slogan: Heritage at Heart, Progress in Mind. It is this balancing act of tradition and modernity that underlies the culture at Mango Bank. Many of its staff feel that the increased adoption of AI and automation are inevitable and fear the imminent changes. Others, more optimistic, feel that how Mango Bank balances this new efficiency with empathy, innovation and inclusivity will define its legacy in years to come.

From the 58th floor, Rupert Wong catches a glimpse of himself in the immaculate glass reflection. He thinks he looks older than usual. A thought crosses his mind . . . what will the bank's leaders of tomorrow be like?

Introducing Kelly and Sofia

In the corridors of Mango Bank, two exceptional women leaders have emerged with distinctly different approaches to leadership and management. Kelly and Sofia, both originally from Malaysia, have managed to climb through the ranks of Mango Bank and challenge the male-dominated hegemony of senior leadership. Their journeys share many parallels but diverge completely in philosophy and approach. Their successes are heralded in the bank as signs of the organisation's commitment to diversity and inclusion initiatives. Both managers get results, but only one of them takes the leadership route.

Kelly

Kelly's journey to the top at Mango Bank might resemble the climb up Malaysia's highest mountain: Mount Kinabalu. A steep ascent full of challenges and not for the faint hearted. Starting in the trenches of Mango Bank's most chaotic departments back in the early 2000s, Kelly quickly realised that chaos was really order waiting to be catalogued. Her early days at Mango Bank were a whirlwind of missing documents, missed deadlines and missed opportunities. Kelly sometimes felt like her office was a kind of corporate Bermuda Triangle where important documents could mysteriously vanish into thin air.

It was into this environment that Kelly's ironclad beliefs in structure and efficiency were formed. Slowly, Kelly was promoted for her in-depth knowledge of the processes and her attention to detail. If a pair of scissors in the office went missing, you could guarantee that Kelly would know where they were! Slowly, she transformed her department into a well-oiled machine that some would describe as part boot camp and part ballet – leaving little room for improvisation and even less room for error. Kelly's general lack of faith in the competence of her subordinates helped her to develop her mantra of 'If you want something done right, do it yourself or stand close enough to ensure it's almost identical.'

Over time, Kelly's attention to detail became legendary. She was famous for her obsession with formatting documents and ensuring that the exact tone of corporate orange (Pantone 151 C, obviously) was used in presentation decks and slides. Famously, Kelly once ran a team-building away day in which her desired outcome from the event wasn't increased trust or empathy but 'a solid understanding' of the Bank's niche processes. Kelly's journey instilled in her the belief that control is not just a management style but a way of life. For Kelly, success was measured in spreadsheets and spontaneity was about as welcome as a porcupine in a balloon factory.

Sofia

Sofia manages her team at Mango Bank with the skills of a seasoned diplomat. Promoted through the ranks for her ability to connect and inspire, Sofia's journey has been equally as challenging as Kelly's. Through these challenges, Sofia learned to reflect and finetune her approach to different people and situations. Some junior staff even refer to Sofia's department as an oasis: a place where collaboration, innovation and even failure are not just tolerated but actively encouraged.

Imagine a workplace where brainstorming sessions and meetings are eagerly anticipated, and laughter often fills the air. Sofia has even been known to kick off meetings with bizarre icebreakers like 'two truths and a lie' about financial trends, or stories of famous Zoom meeting blunders. It's this touch of humour that makes even the most challenging targets feel like a shared adventure.

Under Sofia, autonomy and empowerment are not just management buzzwords – but the cornerstone of her leadership approach. Sofia believes in the potential of her team so much that she once delegated the annual strategic presentation to a group of junior team members. This risky decision helped to showcase that everyone in Sofia's 'oasis' had a voice. The fresh perspective that the junior team members shared also impressed the senior executives so much so that it set a new precedent for trust and inclusion within Mango Bank.

Introduction

Over the past 20 years, my work in learning and development has helped to form my beliefs about leadership and management. Starting my own company 13 years ago and navigating the challenges of building a team and culture with limited resources helped me to translate theory into practice. It certainly wasn't always smooth sailing. *The Leadership Route* is the distillation of those years of trial and error. It is based on the years of learning, failures and growth that have helped me move closer to what I strongly believe effective leadership is in these turbulent times. I have drawn from countless training sessions, coaching conversations, client meetings and even from experimentation with my own company. I hope you see this book as a stepping stone to becoming a more effective leader and manager. But it's not just that. I hope this book provides you with a chance to reflect on your own journey in life. Are you here to conquer or to uplift?

My journey in learning and development was driven by my own 'shy extroversion'. A desire to step out of my comfort zone and to help others do the same. I realised that I was most happy when I was stretching myself and challenging fixed ideas of what I could achieve. It made sense that a career helping others to do the same would drive me: *growing myself whilst growing others.*

Running my training company compounded these beliefs and I started to really understand the concept of engagement. It is a leader's ability to influence and inspire others to challenge themselves that retains talent. Managers and leaders are all about unlocking potential. You might be grinning cynically at this point thinking, you don't manage a team like mine! But bear with me . . . .

Engagement really is the 'secret sauce' or sambal behind effective organisational performance. It's the magic formula that all organisations are looking for. Engagement isn't just about satisfaction; it is about creating a culture where people feel inspired and connected to the mission. It reminds me of that famous janitor at NASA who told President Kennedy he was 'helping put a man on the moon' rather than cleaning floors. Furthermore, my journey has led me to the belief that *everyone* has potential. This often runs contrary to battle hardened managers who profess that certain individuals have 'got what it takes' and that some people are simply 'beyond help'.

In *The Leadership Route*, I want to share with you how I shaped my beliefs. I will present ideas from classic management theory to more modern research based on neuroscience and behavioural and social psychology. This is not an academic book, but I do want to show you how my ideas are backed up by compelling theories and in many cases hard factual evidence.

This book is designed to make you see beyond the bottom line. It's all about helping people to feel safe, seen and motivated to grow. It centres on finding purpose in helping others to grow. Ultimately, I believe that *you only live once, but your legacy can live forever.*

As you read through this book, I encourage you to critically evaluate what you read. I also encourage you to reflect – at the start of each chapter I have included a reflection task that is designed to help you contemplate your current approach. You can then reflect on whether there has been any change in your approach at the end of the chapter by answering the guided reflection questions. My wish is that this book serves as a catalyst for growth, inspiration and positive change in your life.

Welcome to *The Leadership Route.* Let's explore the ideas in this book with an open mind and open heart. I hope that by the end of it, you are as convinced as I am that the leadership route for managers entails lifting others and in so doing uplifting ourselves.

Finally, this book is not a collection of factual stories from the corporate world. Instead, I will draw upon two women leaders, Kelly and Sofia, and their journeys through a fictitious institution: Mango Bank. The bank is a composite of the many organisations I have worked with both in the financial sector and other industries. Mango Bank, like many organisations, is navigating a time of immense change and uncertainty. As organisations and their people grapple with the profound changes that automation and AI are bringing, we will look to Kelly and Sofia to provide two entirely different approaches to managing in turbulent times. Through the lens of Mango Bank, we will examine strategies for fostering an inclusive culture, encouraging innovation and maintaining resilience. We will learn how choosing the 'leadership route' can overcome generational differences and help people feel connected to organisations in a time where people are arguably more disconnected than ever before. Ultimately, we will learn how different approaches to management can shape a leader.

BELIEFS

Treat a man as he is and he will remain as he is. Treat a man as he can and should be, and he will become as he can and should be.

—Stephen Covey

REFLECTION TASK: YOUR BELIEFS

Instructions: Rate each statement on a scale from Strongly Disagree (1) to Strongly Agree (5).

Statement	Strongly Disagree (1)	Disagree (2)	Neutral (3)	Agree (4)	Strongly Agree (5)
1. Most people will seek responsibility rather than avoid it if they are motivated properly.					
2. People mainly work for money and security, and little else motivates them.					
3. Most people have a high degree of imagination and creativity that can be used to solve organisational problems.					
4. Without active intervention by management, work will not get done.					
5. The satisfaction of doing a good job is a strong motivation for most people.					
6. Most people inherently dislike work and will avoid it if they can.					

Statement	Strongly Disagree (1)	Disagree (2)	Neutral (3)	Agree (4)	Strongly Agree (5)
7. People are capable of self-direction and self-control if they are committed to the objectives.					
8. Most people need to be closely supervised and controlled with strict rules to ensure that they complete their tasks.					
9. People become attached to and involved in their work if they feel their job is important and appreciated.					
10. The average person prefers to be directed, wishes to avoid responsibility, has relatively little ambition and wants security above all.					

Read the chapter before you check your answers on p. 259.

It All Begins with Beliefs

Beliefs are the invisible drivers that shape our reality and help drive our decision-making. They are inculcated from childhood and compounded by our experiences. Sometimes, our experiences serve to reinforce our beliefs or lead us to reevaluate things. For leaders and managers, our beliefs may stem from how we were managed ourselves. Perhaps how we were 'managed' by our parents. As these beliefs fossilise, they become our personal guiding principles. Over time, these same principles become the compasses that steer entire organisations, influence team dynamics and ultimately decide the success or failure of all our efforts. It all begins with beliefs.

This chapter explores the influence that beliefs have on our attitudes to leadership and management. It explores how the convictions we have about ourselves, work and human nature manifest in our management style, our approaches to creativity and problem-solving and our ability to influence and inspire those around us. We might not be aware of it, but our beliefs influence every aspect of our management approach, from how we delegate tasks to how we give feedback or even recognition. This chapter will help you evaluate whether the beliefs you have are conducive to the leadership route and the path of lifting others.

We will return to our two protagonists, Kelly and Sofia, and explore how the beliefs of each manager can shape the climate of a workplace, the morale of a team and the trajectory of a career. Through their stories, we will discover that beliefs can act as both bridges and barriers. Bridges to uplift and lead us to people-centric and innovative leadership, or barriers that can constrain us to limit the potential of our people and our organisation.

I think it is important to remember that beliefs are not static. In fact, beliefs are malleable constructs that can be changed through reflection, new experiences and by being open to fresh perspectives. Everything begins with beliefs and so the evolution of our beliefs will ultimately be the evolution of our leadership.

Kelly

Kelly holds the reins of Mango Bank's International Operations division. It's a position some would compare to captaining a ship through the Straits of Malacca – one of the busiest shipping lanes in the world. It's an environment that is challenging and unpredictable – requiring an unshakeable sense of direction. Kelly's management style resembles a chess grandmaster. Except that every pawn on the board is a critical project and the knights are her direct reports. With Kelly, every move on the board requires precision and careful planning.

In Kelly's world, spontaneity is the enemy of order. Meetings in her team are conducted with the precision of an orchestral symphony. Every person must play their part at the right time. Kelly's detail focus is legendary. It is even rumoured she once gave a workshop on the optimum number of icons on a desktop for efficiency, a workshop that is spoken about in hushed tones around the bank's water dispensers.

Kelly's belief in oversight and control to maintain the bank's high standards and to achieve ambitious targets are equally infamous. She operates with the assumption that without her vigilant eye, things could well descend into chaos.

All of this has led her to develop a system of metrics, reports and meetings that could rival the complexity of a space shuttle launch.

When it comes to motivation, Kelly uses intricate reward systems that include monetary bonuses as well as more unusual rewards like lunch with the CFO and a day shadowing a department of their choice (as long as they write a full report on it within 48 hours). Alternatively, her approach to underperformance makes even a seasoned Mango Banker shudder involuntarily. Her performance improvement plans are known to be as detailed as they are daunting.

How do her team cope? Kelly's team manage the high seas of Operations with a mixture of fear, respect and a robust sense of humour. However, there's a deep sense that, although their pay is good, they might be missing out on something. As more and more talented team members leave, Kelly holds fast to the belief that not everyone is cut out for the treacherous waters of Operations.

Sofia

Sofia's domain in retail banking is vast and her team covers multiple countries and cultures. Driven by the same ambitious strategy as Kelly, Sofia takes a different approach. Her 'oasis' is a place where the rigorous demands of the financial sector are met by a large but tight-knit family. People know each other on first name terms and mistakes are seen as stepping stones to success. When a high-stakes project hits a snag, Sofia gathers her team around her and says: 'Well, we've found one way that doesn't work. Let's find the one that does'.

Her debrief sessions turn into fun problem-solving workshops where even the most introvert members share their ideas.

Recognition in Sofia's team comes in many forms. There are traditional bonuses and rewards as well as the more unusual 'innovator of the month' award, which involves a trophy made from recycled materials. It's not uncommon to hear team members playfully negotiating for the trophy, a symbol of Sofia's culture of encouragement and appreciation.

Sofia's 'oasis' thrives on the notion that when people feel trusted, included and connected they can achieve extraordinary things. Her leadership style may be unconventional in the fast-paced world of international finance, but her results speak for themselves. Under her guidance, her team achieve incredible stretch goals with a spirit of camaraderie and innovation that has become the envy of the bank.

Above all, team members are loyal to Sofia and her team. Many have stayed for years and those that leave are always complimentary to her and the team. A quick website search will find employees pouring out their praise for Sofia and her 'oasis', a shining example of how employee experience goes beyond perks and benefits.

A Tale of Two Managers – Theory X and Y

In the 1960s a US social psychologist named Douglas McGregor posited a theory that challenged traditional beliefs about managing people. The idea was a more optimistic and inspirational set of beliefs compared to traditional Taylorism, which was focused on efficiency and people being seen as 'cogs in a machine'.[1] McGregor developed the idea of Theory X and Y[2] managers based on his insights as a psychologist and educator (see Figure 1). The theory suggests that the traditional Taylorist set of beliefs – Theory X – leads to a more controlling management style. The other – Theory Y – leads managers to a more collaborative and empowering approach.

Perhaps you might think that a lot has changed since the 1960s, but if you recognise the stories of Kelly and Sofia, you might have some idea of how relevant this theory is even today. My company's work with thousands of individuals and many organisations has also revealed how much the dichotomy between Theory X and Y prevails today.

Kelly's management style illustrates a Theory X leader. Theory X leaders inherently distrust people to work effectively and believe that they are mostly motivated by fear and financial gain. *I have always been surprised by the number of participants in my training sessions who still share this belief!* Theory X leaders also believe that most people lack creativity and avoid responsibility. Think of the type of manager who worries everyone in their office will be checking their Instagram or TikTok instead of working the moment they leave the room. Theory X beliefs drive Kelly's behaviour of close supervision, stringent rules and the need for a clear hierarchy of authority. This approach is also heavily skewed towards control through financial rewards and punishment – the classic 'carrot-and-stick' approach.

Sofia's approach embodies the Theory Y manager. This type of manager believes that humans inherently need and want to work if the conditions are favourable. It also suggests that managers who are Theory Y are more likely to believe that people are creative and open to responsibility if they have some autonomy. This optimistic view of human nature leads to a management style that emphasises empowerment and a partnership between managers and employees. Sofia's leadership style is characterised by her trust in her team's capability, encouragement of autonomy and a belief in the power of intrinsic motivation. Theory Y suggests that work can be as natural as play if the right conditions, which foster engagement, creativity and a sense of belonging, are in place.

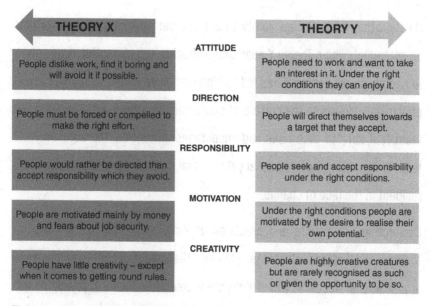

Figure 1: Theory X and Y beliefs

But you might argue, Kelly's style *is* effective in getting results. Indeed, Kelly's success in meeting financial targets and fine-tuning operational efficiency demonstrate that Theory X can be effective in environments where control and consistency are paramount. However, Kelly's approach also leads to high staff turnover as people feel stifled and are unable to grow. Furthermore, the lack of spontaneity and innovation are likely to limit the long-term sustainability of her department as new ideas are not championed and results are almost always efficiency driven. The focus on control also limits her team's 'change adaptability' in the face of organisational shifts – a competence that most organisations need right now. After all, when we are so used to being told what to do and how to do it, it can be terrifying when we don't have that immediate guidance or sense of certainty.

On the other hand, Sofia's ability to achieve her stretch goals and targets despite employing a Theory Y approach highlights the strengths of this style. Her focus on engagement has led to high employee loyalty and lower levels of attrition. Moreover, the culture of continuous improvement also helps her team feel safe to take risks and encourages innovation. The autonomy her team feels with this professional yet informal culture also makes them more resilient in the face of change.

Connecting the beliefs and practices of Kelly and Sofia to the ideas of Theory X and Y offers valuable insights into the impact of beliefs on team and organisational success. Whilst Kelly's adherence to Theory X principles has brought about operational success, it has also revealed the limitations of a management style that is rooted in control and relies upon extrinsic motivation (rewards and punishment). In contrast, Sofia's style demonstrates how results can be maintained albeit with a softer more empathetic style, focused on autonomy, intrinsic motivation and a collaborative culture. Figure 2 shows the long-term impacts of Theory X and Y.

IMPACT OF THEORY X	IMPACT OF THEORY Y
Decreased Employee Morale	Increased Engagement
Limited Employee Development	Enhanced Employee Development
High Attrition	Higher Retention
Lack of Innovation and Creativity	Foster Innovation and Creativity
Resistance to Change	Adaptability to Change
Limited Employee Loyalty	Enhanced Organisational Reputation

Figure 2: Long-term impact of Theory X and Y

Theory Z

You might ask — is there a third approach, a middle ground? So did William Ouchi, an American Japanese professor. In the 1980s, Ouchi developed Theory Z as a hybrid of both Theory X and Y,[3] with influences from Japanese management approaches. Theory Z emphasises long-term employment, collective decision-making and individual responsibility within a stable workplace. It aimed to create an environment that fosters both loyalty and productivity.

Theory Z offers a caring context where managers are concerned for their employees both inside and outside the workplace. This is an idea that I think is very valuable as we progress further in the book. Essentially, Theory Z works on the idea that through care and concern for our employees we can maintain high levels of commitment, loyalty and satisfaction whilst maintaining a structured and organised work environment.

Theory Y and Lifting

While Theory Z offers a balanced approach that incorporates both Theory X and Y, I feel that Theory Y still offers the more suitable approach for leaders who aim to take the leadership route by 'lifting' others. This is especially important in the context of today's technology-driven and knowledge-based workforce. The following are the reasons why I feel this is the case:

Innovation and creativity: Theory Y has a focus on individual contributions and a culture of autonomy that are more likely to produce disruptive ideas and innovation. With Theory Z's focus on harmony and collective decision-making it may be more challenging to generate really breakthrough ideas.

Resilience and adaptability: With its focus on continuous learning, Theory Y encourages employees to adapt and reskill, making the organisation more prepared for change when needed. In contrast, Theory Z's emphasis on stability over learning may lead to stagnation and apathy.

Job satisfaction and retention: As team members (like in Sofia's team) feel like they are growing and being pushed out of their comfort zone, they are more likely to be engaged and stay with the organisation. If the focus is on security (Theory Z), it may develop a 'work for the paycheque' culture where employees are satisfied but not engaged.

Collaboration: When managers trust their employees through empowerment, they build a more collaborative culture where team members feel their contributions are recognised through increased responsibility and autonomy.

Nevertheless, Theory Z, and its paternalistic style, offers some valuable advice for managers who want to lead by lifting. The focus on care and concern for team members' welfare is an important one. After all, if we want to evaluate whether an employee's emotional well-being has been impacted by factors outside work, it is essential that managers are aware of what is happening to their team members *outside* work.

The Power of Beliefs – Two Fables

The 1960s might seem like a long time ago. But let's rewind even further to explore two ideas from mythology. These two myths were used by psychologists to illustrate the power of beliefs on outcomes.

THE PYGMALION EFFECT

Pygmalion was a sculptor in Greek mythology who wanted to find the perfect woman. As a result, he set to work crafting an amazingly beautiful woman from ivory. It was a vision of perfection. So much so that, the Goddess of Love – Aphrodite – brought her to life. But what has this got to do with Kelly and Sofia or Theory X and Y? Well, the Pygmalion effect was discovered by psychologists Robert Rosenthal and Lenore Jacobson in 1968,[4] where their research showed that teachers who believed their students were more capable than past results suggested, performed better. Similarly, managers and leaders who trust their team's potential may be able to help them achieve higher levels of performance. Sofia's high expectations and trust in her team's abilities act as a catalyst for higher performance. Literally bringing expectation to life, as Pygmalion did with his statue.

THE GOLEM EFFECT

The Golem effect is based on an ancient story from Jewish mythology. The Golem was a mythical creature brought to life through magic and created from mud or clay. The Golem's role would be to protect its master or the community. Unfortunately, the Golem would often become uncontrollable and cause harm. The Golem effect is the flipside of Pygmalion[5] and illustrates that low expectations from leaders can lead to decreased performance in employees. Kelly's lack of trust and her belief that she needs to do everything herself suppresses performance. Her beliefs that other people need constant supervision in turn will make people *seek* constant supervision. Her fear is that given power, her team will turn into a bunch of Golems — not a good look for Operations at Mango Bank!

Many children when they grow up face the Pygmalion or Golem effect from their parents or teachers. While some children will rebel against the assumptions that they have potential or not, many adopt these limiting beliefs from their parents. As managers who take the leadership route, we must understand that if we believe in our team and their potential, they are more likely to rise to the challenge.

MASLOW, HERZBERG AND LIFTING

The leadership route of lifting also aligns with the motivation theories of Maslow and Herzberg (and Csikszentmihalyi — but we will discuss his theory later). Abraham Maslow's wonderful hierarchy of needs[6] and Frederick Herzberg's two-factor theory[7] both confirm McGregor's optimism. Maslow's theory stated that the hierarchy of needs started with basic physiological needs like food and water. But on top of the hierarchy were esteem and self-actualisation (the need to fulfil potential). Similarly, Herzberg suggested that some factors led to general satisfaction (the lower-order motivators in Maslow's hierarchy) while other factors led to engagement. He called factors that led to general satisfaction — hygiene factors and those which led to engagement – motivators. The lower-order 'hygiene factors' include company policy, work–life balance and even personal life. Interestingly, Herzberg suggested that salary was a hygiene factor and not a motivator! Many participants in my training challenge this idea.

In 2018, *Harvard Business Review* conducted a study in which they found 9 out of 10 people were willing to earn less to do more 'meaningful work'.[8] Many senior leaders that I have spoken to corroborate this idea. Many have enough money to retire comfortably but continue working. They always tell me what keeps them going is challenge, recognition and legacy (motivators). Later in this book we will also find out how neuroscience itself reinforces this theory. Figure 3 illustrates how Maslow's hierarchy maps onto Herzberg and Theory X and Y.

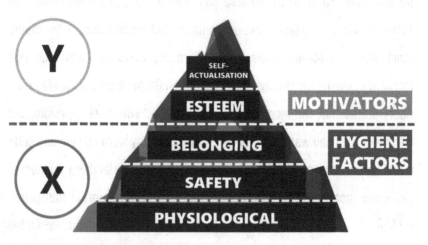

Figure 3: Maslow, Herzberg and Theory X and Y

Kelly's reliance on extrinsic rewards connects with Maslow's lower-order needs and hygiene factors. This might mean she is limiting the potential of her team to be engaged at work. Employees who feel trapped by a lack of career choices, financial necessity or fear of change will stay with Kelly but are unlikely to feel truly engaged and ultimately happy.

Sofia's approach, focused more on the higher-order needs and motivators, is more likely to inspire her team to greatness (provided they feel they have the hygiene factors in place). When you are aligned with purpose and growth, people need less money, work harder and are more engaged.

THEORY X IN THE AGE OF TECH

As organisations continue to automate routine tasks and factory-type processes, the need for strict control by managers is being reduced. The future of work will involve creative problem-solving and leveraging empathy. It will likely revolve around effective communication and critical thinking.

Some of the interesting comments I often hear from managers are: 'my team never takes any risks', or 'they don't take ownership of their work' and 'I'm not getting any innovative ideas.' When I hear this, I wonder whether these managers are still too Theory X – still focused on control when they need to start taking the leadership route and lifting.

LIFTING IN THE AGE OF TECH

Managers are often promoted to become managers because of their superior skill at a given task. For example, a manager who could answer more calls and resolve more complaints would often be promoted in a call centre. However, that same manager would often struggle with people management skills that they had never really been taught. As a result, the manager would fall back on their competence in their skill and adopt a controlling style of management – often intimidated by the potential of their peers. However, as we move into the age of tech, managers are going to be working with teams who have more knowledge and skill than they do.[9] Employees have access to vast amounts of information through the internet and artificial intelligence, giving them the power to be more autonomous than ever before. Managers who attempt to lead through control will simply lose talented individuals to more aspiring organisations.

Organisations are also becoming flatter and more agile. This transformation is taking place not just in tech companies but in government organisations. As organisations realise they need to get flatter to be more connected to their customers, they are becoming less hierarchical, and managers are less able to pull on conventional position power.

Thus, taking the leadership route is not a choice but a necessity in the modern workplace. As generation Z becomes more present at work, they will be looking for leaders who can inspire and connect. A study by Deloitte in 2023 found that Gen Z employees prioritise flexibility, inclusivity and purpose.[10] When Theory X leaders lead Gen Z employees, they might moan about them lacking a work ethic or loyalty. But Gen Z may have the greatest solutions for our era as they were born in an age of unprecedented information power.

Finally, as we move towards remote work and new ways of working, Theory X will become more challenging to enforce. We will need to learn to trust and inspire. Work will need to be truly engaging for employees to resist the temptations that lurk at home.

Kelly and Sofia exemplify the two different routes that managers can take in their own stories. Kelly's Theory X approach is still arguably the most pervasive management approach used today. From manufacturing to governments, we all know a 'Kelly'. And a 'Kelly' isn't always a bad thing. Sometimes, we need Kellys in compliance-driven workplaces or organisations with rigid hierarchies. But would we ever call Kelly our inspiration? Would we think of her long after we have retired and be tempted to send her a text message? Sofia, who seems to challenge us to be the best we can be, is tomorrow's leader. She knows that people need to be engaged to truly perform. She understands that true loyalty comes from respect and not fear.

Chapter Echo

As Rupert Wong ponders over what the leaders of tomorrow look like, he considers how leadership presented itself when he was a junior manager. He remembers the fear of meeting deadlines, how terrified he was of his old boss and the abject terror he had of some of the Board members. He recollects the siloes and the office politics that seemed to get in the way of new ideas and real change. As he looks out over the futuristic landscape of Singapore, the thought hits him: does the Bank really have progress in mind?

Key Takeaways – Chapter One

1. Beliefs as Foundations

- Beliefs are the core elements shaping manager actions, decisions and interactions.
- They influence perceptions, choices and the way managers interact with their teams and organisations.

2. Impact of Beliefs on Leadership Styles

- Management styles are a reflection of underlying beliefs about oneself, the team and the nature of work.
- These beliefs manifest in management styles, problem-solving approaches and the capacity to inspire and motivate.

3. Theory X and Theory Y

- Theory X
  - Assumes employees are inherently lazy and need constant supervision.
  - Relies on control and extrinsic motivation.

- **Theory Y**

  - Assumes employees are intrinsically motivated and capable of self-direction.

  - Emphasises empowerment, trust and intrinsic motivation.

4. Introducing Theory Z

- Combines elements of Theory X and Theory Y, with a focus on long-term employment and collective decision-making.

- Balances control and autonomy, fostering loyalty and productivity.

5. Pygmalion and Golem Effects

- **Pygmalion effect**

  - High expectations from leaders lead to improved performance.

- **Golem effect**

  - Low expectations from leaders lead to decreased performance.

6. Maslow's Hierarchy of Needs and Herzberg's Two-Factor Theory

- **Maslow**

  - Human actions are motivated by a hierarchy of needs, from basic to self-actualisation.

- **Herzberg**

  - Divides motivational factors into hygiene factors (prevent dissatisfaction) and motivators (generate engagement).

- Focusing on lower-level needs and hygiene factors can prevent dissatisfaction but may not enhance engagement.

- Tapping into higher-level needs and motivators fosters long-term satisfaction and motivation.

7. The Carrot-and-Stick Model

- This model assumes motivation is primarily driven by external rewards and punishments.

- Maslow and Herzberg's theories reveal that true motivation is more complex and involves intrinsic factors.

8. Leadership Evolution

- Beliefs are malleable and can change through reflection, experience and embracing new perspectives.

- Understanding and evolving beliefs is essential for becoming a leader who lifts and transforms.

9. Practical Application

- Managers should reflect on their own beliefs and how they impact their management style.

- By adopting a people-centric approach and focusing on intrinsic motivators, leaders can create more innovative, engaged and resilient teams.

Reflection Questions

- Where do your beliefs about managing people come from?

- Are these beliefs helping you and the people around you to grow?

SAFETY

For knowledge work to flourish, the workplace must be one where people feel able to share their knowledge!

—Amy Edmondson

REFLECTION TASK: MINDSET

Instructions: Rate each statement on a scale from Strongly Disagree (1) to Strongly Agree (5).

Statement	Strongly Disagree (1)	Disagree (2)	Neutral (3)	Agree (4)	Strongly Agree (5)
1. Challenges are opportunities for growth and development.					
2. Intelligence and talent are fixed traits and cannot be developed over time.					
3. Feedback is essential for improving performance and should be actively sought.					
4. People are either naturally good at tasks or not, and there's little they can do to change that.					
5. Effort and perseverance are more important than inherent talent for success.					
6. It's important to avoid failure at all costs to maintain a positive image.					

Statement	Strongly Disagree (1)	Disagree (2)	Neutral (3)	Agree (4)	Strongly Agree (5)
7. Employees can significantly improve their skills with practice and dedication.					
8. Only a few employees have the potential to become top performers.					
9. Learning from mistakes is a crucial part of the growth process.					
10. When faced with a setback, the best approach is to give up and try something else.					

Read the chapter before you check your answers on p. 260

Safety

If we want our teams to be engaged, they need to feel safe. As we explored with Maslow's hierarchy, safety is a fundamental need for employees. Without safety, employees are unable to complete the higher-order tasks in Maslow's hierarchy. They are removed from Herzberg's hygiene factors and are therefore unable to be truly engaged.

Safety means, of course, freedom from abuse or bullying by managers or other employees. It is important to remember that safety does not only encompass the physiological. Managers often forget that safety depends on how others evaluate threats, and this is often being monitored at a subconscious level. We might refer to it as *psychological safety*.

Psychological safety at work is a term that was popularised by Amy Edmonson, in her seminal book *The Fearless Organization*.[1] It refers to an organisational climate in which employees feel free to express their feelings and thoughts without being punished or marginalised. Safety is pivotal in organisations as employees who feel safe are more likely to be engaged. If you feel safe, you are more likely to share your ideas, and this can help lead to innovation and organisational growth.

Google's famous Project Aristotle also underscores the importance of psychological safety.[2] In the project, researchers identified that psychological safety was the most significant factor distinguishing high-performing teams. The research identified that teams with high levels of psychological safety were more likely to generate innovative ideas, identify errors quickly without fear of punishment and remain resilient in the face of challenges. But Google is Google I hear you say! Well, do you want your organisation or team to be innovative, resilient and dare I say – agile? If the answer is yes, then psychological safety can help managers develop team members who attempt to challenge the status quo, question decisions, critically evaluate, problem-solve and take smart risks. All because they feel safe. If you fear retribution from your manager for questioning long-held assumptions, chances are you will stay firmly within your comfort zone – working for your pay cheque.

Psychological safety can be embedded in the processes of how we manage and lead others. It can be inculcated in organisational culture and leaders need to role model this for others. We need to encourage others to feel safe enough to reach their potential – even if this means falling short. Managers need to shift from command and control to a more empathetic style of leadership. Leaders who 'lift' are likely to adopt this style as they are aware that we need to feel safe to be truly authentic. The quiet and reserved employee may be bubbling with creative ideas below the surface and just needs the chance to share these ideas free from the fear of ridicule or judgement. Many team members may have some form of trauma from school where they were laughed at for speaking up or challenging convention. *Get over it you might say*. Well, your work as a manager is to help them do exactly that: by building a safe space.

In this chapter, we draw on ideas from neuroscience to help us understand how people perceive threats at work. We will also learn the power of growth – something we need to embody as managers and leaders.

Let us return to the stories of Kelly and Sofia, and their work within Mango Bank – poised on the cusp of change.

KELLY

Kelly's command-and-control style at Mango Bank resembles a military commander with her laser-focused attention to efficiency and detail. However, her approach often results in unintended consequences that leave her team feeling puzzled and sometimes bemused.

For example, during a particular quarterly targets meeting, Kelly once decided to set the goals and targets single handedly without consulting her team. Her reasoning was that only *she* knew the bigger picture and that this was the fastest route to success. By overlooking her team's input, Kelly missed the chance to benefit from their valuable insights. But she *did* feel powerful! Sadly, the same could not be said for her team. Picture them sitting around the conference table, staring blankly at Kelly and feeling as involved as a lizard at a cat show.

When giving feedback, Kelly doesn't pull any punches. She would often be reminded of her grandmother's saying that 'good medicine tastes bitter to the mouth' and would dish out critical feedback like a waiter would throw noodles onto her plate at her favourite street-food stall.

Kelly also likes to stick to plans despite emerging risks. She is like a pilot insisting on flying through a storm because that was the 'course we charted'. When things get turbulent, she is always about sticking to the plan without even letting her team know to expect a bumpy ride – business as usual without switching the seatbelt sign on. This is frustrating for her team who often have ready-to-go insights to share and solutions that require minor modifications to plans. Once when Navin, a senior manager, cautiously knocked on her door to suggest that there were major risks to a project rollout, Kelly infamously opened her door and stated, 'if you are not bringing me solutions – I don't want to hear it!'

Kelly also values hierarchy in her team, clearly assigning more challenging tasks based on seniority whilst more junior team members receive less critical duties. This not only limits the growth of talent in her team but creates a profound sense of unfairness. Juniors grumble about favouritism whilst senior members wonder if they are being overburdened. In line with her adherence to hierarchy, Kelly hates more junior employees approaching her without first speaking to their supervisors or line managers. She might find herself staring blankly at a more junior team member: 'what's your name again?', she would ask before demanding who their line manager was and gentling shooing them back to the respective person.

When changes happen in the organisation, Kelly holds onto the information from Senior Leaders like a squirrel might hold onto a peanut at the onset of winter. When there is uncertainty and her team ask for updates, Kelly will promptly respond: 'I really don't know, why don't you ask Rupert?!'. Once, when a major restructuring happened in the Bank, Kelly held onto this power, using uncertainty as a tool to motivate her team. 'Be thankful!', she would declare 'Many people don't have any work right now!'.

Despite her best intentions, Kelly often leaves her team feeling undervalued and disconnected. While they recognise that they *are* indeed lucky to have work, they can't help feeling like they are missing out. Even at home, they are never fully free from the tentacles of Kelly who might suddenly appear in their WhatsApp messages with a forwarded communication from an angry client or an urgent request for a meeting.

SOFIA

In Sofia's oasis, things are done differently. When Sofia walks briskly into the office, she greets the security guards and cleaners by name, often asking one of the security guards how their son is. Her energy is contagious as she bursts into the office greeting her team and heading to her desk in the middle of the room.

Inside the office, Sofia is usually visible huddled around a group of employees listening to their ideas intently. Other times, Sofia is seen standing at the window quietly sipping jasmine tea and looking into the distance, deep in thought. Sometimes, you might even hear Sofia telling a story of a bad decision she made or a flopped project to a group of new recruits, drawing laughter.

Sofia routinely involves her team in important decisions, openly discussing strategies and targets and bringing her team up to speed with any big picture downloads she has received from further up. As a result, her team can connect even the smallest tasks to the customer and in turn to the organisation's success. Every cog is vital.

Meetings in Sofia's oasis resemble productive coffee breaks albeit with fewer cookies and more charts. No ideas are ridiculed and even the most outrageous of suggestions is met with intense interest. This creative approach is reflected in how she tackles challenges. Sofia turns potential setbacks into moments of creativity, like turning lemons into lemonade, but with a touch of corporate flair. Junior team members are often surprised that Sofia can remember their names and even more so when she remembers their ideas. Even more unusually, Sofia encourages members to take the initiative when they see an opportunity. She's often heard talking to her team about the importance of leveraging both analytical thinking and that often-overlooked tool: gut. Head and heart. Yin and yang.

When major changes are cascaded down from the top, Sofia lets her team know clearly about uncertainties and is always quick to provide a date or time when she will give her team an update – even if that update is only to state when the next update is!

Above all, Sofia tries to create opportunities for everyone to contribute and lead based on their strengths. She ensures that achievements are recognised and gives praise freely. She's even the first in WhatsApp chats to congratulate her team members for their hard work after a successful project, taking care to praise both equally and frequently. When things go wrong, Sofia attempts to help her team members identify what they could do better next time rather than simply imparting her own experience or drawing on her expertise.

As a result of her inclusive style, Sofia doesn't have her team clenching their teeth or gripping the armrests of their chairs every time she comes into the room. In fact, she minimises threats whilst cultivating a deep respect and admiration in her followers. Her approach makes her team feel a bit like they are the cast of a hit Netflix series, where everyone knows their part and every character plays a starring role.

SCARF

Many managers unconsciously make their team members feel psychologically unsafe at work. Because of this, team members feel threatened and perform at far less capacity than they are capable of. They become *disengaged*. So, what can managers do to make their teams feel safer and perform better? We turn here to the SCARF model and the work of Dr David Rock, the co-founder and CEO of the Neuroleadership Institute.[3] His research on the human brain based on scans discovered a powerful revelation. He observed that the human brain would respond to certain social interactions with a reward-or-threat response. Dr Rock wove together multiple studies and came up with five key domains: the SCARF model. A bit like wearing a scarf to protect us from the cold, managers would do well to use the SCARF model to protect their teams from unnecessary threats and to cultivate psychological safety. The SCARF model stands for:

Status: our status or relative importance in relation to others.

Certainty: our ability to predict the future.

Autonomy: a sense of control over our lives.

Relatedness: our sense of connection and similarity to others.

Fairness: how we perceive a fair exchange between people

By being aware of these domains, we can help to keep people in a state of engagement rather than in a threat state. A particularly interesting finding from the study was that praise would light up the same part of the brain as receiving a monetary reward. The only difference being that praise would elicit a higher response from the brain. Could this be scientific evidence that money really is a less powerful motivator than we think it is? Perhaps. Another interesting finding was that people who received constructive feedback (being told what they could do better) would lead to a threat response in the brain that mirrored physical pain. Could managers be accidentally hurting their team through feedback? Let's go back for a moment to the stories of Kelly and Sofia and see how they influence their team by connecting their stories to SCARF.

Kelly – A Cautionary Tale

Kelly's Theory X approach to management, rooted in traditional hierarchical management, often undermines the SCARF principles. Her focus on strict control and oversight might often impact her team's sense of *autonomy*. This leaves her team members experiencing a threat response that, over time, could lead to disengagement.

Kelly's lack of empowerment and off-the-cuff remarks also undermine her team's sense of *status*. Her critical feedback will undoubtedly leave her team feeling threatened. Sometimes, when we give people direct feedback, have you noticed that they will argue with us? This is them responding to that threat and becoming defensive. They may perceive that we as managers are trying to undermine them to maintain our control. How very Theory X of us!

Kelly also impacts *certainty*. Her lack of transparency with information during periods of change leaves her team feeling anxious. Moreover, her need to hold on to important information and use uncertainty as a tool of control to make herself seem powerful masks her own inner fears.

Kelly inadvertently affects the *fairness* domain through delegation. Her approach might seem fair to her, but ironically is perceived as unfair by both junior and more senior team members.

Finally, Kelly seems to care little about *relatedness*. Her attempts to portray herself as the perfect leader inadvertently make her unrelatable. She doesn't connect with her team on a personal level and permeates every aspect of their life in a threatening way.

Kelly doesn't necessarily mean to make her team feel unsafe. Perhaps she feels that driving her team is the best way to get results and this involves 'tough love' and hard conversations. But unwittingly, Kelly is creating a climate of fear in her team and whilst this might make her team jump to work when she glides into the office to check on them – it doesn't make them engaged.

Sofia – SCARF in Action

Sofia embodies the principles of SCARF in how she interacts with her team. This leaves her team feeling included, valued and engaged.

By genuinely listening to ideas from her team, Sofia elevates their sense of *status*. After all, there is nothing like being truly listened to to make you feel valued! She also offers regular praise through her chat groups ensuring that she praises often. When we remind people of what they do well and their value, they are so much more likely to be in a reward state. Sofia also raises the status of her team members by remembering their names and ideas.

Sofia offers *certainty* in how she shares expectations and minimises ambiguity. She handles change by being proactive and ensuring that her team has anchors amid uncertainty. In addition, as everyone knows their role in the team, expectations are clear, and team members are aware of how they connect to the bigger picture.

As she encourages her team to lead and make their own decisions, Sofia safeguards their sense of *autonomy*. This helps them feel like they have control over their outcomes and is a vital part of helping people develop a sense of engagement. Sofia's encouraging of risk – taking is also a vital part of engagement. Risk is stepping outside the comfort zone and is an essential ingredient for growth. Without risk, there is no growth.

Sofia fosters a sense of *relatedness* with her team through a more informal approach. She positions herself as fallible and that in turn makes her more relatable. Rather than making herself perfect, Sofia makes herself relatable and vulnerable.

Finally, Sofia attempts to stay *fair* as much as she can. Her focus on giving recognition fairly and offering her entire team opportunities to lead also helps her team perceive her as fair.

Sofia ensures that her team feel safe with her. She pays attention to the domains of SCARF and is far more likely to have her team engaged and capable of high performance. She is following the leadership route and leading by lifting.

SCARF AND LIFTING

Through the lens of SCARF, we can observe the stark difference in approach between Kelly and Sofia. Kelly may seem effective as she drives her team towards results through strict control and clear lines of command. And Kelly gets results. But is she really maximising the potential of her team? Sofia on the other hand makes her team feel safe and valued. As Dr Rock himself says, 'when you use SCARF, you are doing things that will generate the reward state – literally making people smarter, more effective, more engaged, and more productive in the workplace.' Literally lifting people.

Growth

Enter another powerful concept: the growth mindset. Carol Dweck's compelling work on the growth mindset[4] and the human capacity to achieve success through a focus on effort has important implications for the leadership route. The growth mindset suggests that talents and abilities are malleable, honed through persistence, taking on challenges and by reframing failure. Dweck incapsulates the growth mindset with the powerful phrase: 'becoming is better than being'. Learning is a continuous state and that when we stop learning we develop a fixed mindset. In its most spiritual sense, a fixed mindset is our attachment to ego and sense of who we are, rather than embracing the fact that who we are is constantly changing. As the US psychologist Daniel Gilbert states, 'human beings are works in progress that mistakenly think they are finished'.[5]

Neuroscience backs up Dweck's ideas through the concept of neuroplasticity: the brain's ability to form new neural connections throughout life. This plasticity allows the brain to adapt to new experiences, learn new skills and recover from injury.

Dweck's work also purports that hard work beats talent. We might do well to remember Thomas Edison, one of history's most prolific inventors, who struggled in school and was labelled as difficult but went on to invent the light bulb.[6] We might think of Jack Ma, who failed the entrance exam for a teacher's college twice and was even rejected for a job at KFC and subsequently created Alibaba Group – one of the world's most successful ecommerce platforms.[7] Perhaps, those of us who equate academic prowess with success, would do well to think of Akio Morita, the co-founder of Sony Corporation who struggled with many subjects and was considered an average student.[8] There are countless examples of hard work beating talent.

On the flipside, we might look at the classic example of William James Sidis who was born in New York in 1898.[9] By the age of two, Sidis was reading the *New York Times* and had managed to learn eight languages, including Latin, Greek, French and Russian. Sidis was accepted to Harvard, aged 11, where he even went on to give lectures on mathematics to students and professors. A real child prodigy. Fast forward to his 40s and Sidis failed to repeat the level of prominence or intellectual productivity he had shown as a child. He died at the age of 46 in relative obscurity and remains a fascinating example of untapped potential and missed opportunities.

But what does all this have to do with different approaches to managing people?

Growth and Lifting

Leaders who lead by Theory X often have a fixed mindset. They are often attached to their identity as being smarter or more effective at tasks than their peers. After all, as we explored earlier, many employees are promoted to be managers solely based on being better at a task than their peers. This 'best in class mindset' often inherited from school or academic excellence *can* lead managers to cling on to this title. As such, managers lead through control and by stifling their team's potential. This fear of being upstaged by their peers limits the growth of employees and teams. Conversely, managers who position themselves as learners are more likely to feel secure around their peers. In fact, they are willing to learn from them and encourage them to grow. Like Sofia, sharing her mistakes and vulnerabilities, these leaders model a growth mindset. They encourage risk taking and experimentation in others and facilitate safe excursions outside our comfort zone. I wonder if Sidis had not been pushed so hard and put on such an enormous pedestal as a child, whether he could have been capable of sharing incredible insights later in life? Perhaps his name would be as famous as Einstein or Edison.

Growing with SCARF

If we feel safe, we are more likely to take risks and experiment. Managers must be wary of whether they promote a reward or danger state in others. Team members need to feel safe to explore new ideas, challenge old ideas, admit mistakes and express themselves freely without fear of reprisal.

Managers can model resilience and a growth mindset by sharing their own stories of failure and how they emerged stronger, thus underscoring the importance of perseverance and adaptability. In fact, they can help to promote a culture that normalises failure, thus encouraging their teams to see setback as a springboard for further development.

GROWTH STRATEGIES

Strategies for inculcating growth mindsets in employees might include:

Celebrating effort and progress: Managers can acknowledge and praise incremental progress rather than just end results. This can help foster a culture where the process is valued: becoming rather than being.

Normalising failure: Managers can normalise failure by reframing setbacks as an essential step in the learning process.

Promoting lifelong learning: Managers should be learners themselves and share their shortcomings with their teams. They should listen intently and avoid overfocusing on their past successes.

Modelling resilience: Managers should exemplify resilience in the face of challenge. They need to role model that perseverance is essential for team and organisational success.

GROWING SAFELY

By marrying the principles of SCARF with the concept of the growth mindset, managers and leaders can build teams where people are safe to innovate and embrace challenge. When team members feel like they are growing (self-actualising) they are more likely to stay engaged and perform at their best. The greatest reward a leader can have is seeing the growth of their team.

Chapter Echo

Rupert Wong, seated now at his expansive director's table, glances at a photo on his desk. His daughter, Carmen, smiling intensely as she holds up her winner's trophy at school. He remembers the fun times playing with her as a little girl, free and full of curiosity. How they would experiment with different games and laugh when they failed. They had grown apart. Looking at that photo it suddenly strikes Rupert . . . maybe he had pushed her too hard? Perhaps he had focused too much on exams and tests. Suddenly, the phone rings and his thoughts are interrupted.

Key Takeaways – Chapter Two

1. **Psychological Safety in the Workplace**

   - Psychological safety goes beyond physical safety, creating an environment where employees feel free to express thoughts and feelings without fear of penalty or marginalisation.
   - It is foundational to employee engagement, innovation and effective problem-solving.

2. **Importance of Psychological Safety**

   - Rooted in Maslow's Hierarchy of Needs, psychological safety supports higher states of well-being and actualisation.
   - Research, such as Google's Project Aristotle, highlights psychological safety as a critical factor in high-performing teams.

3. Management's Role in Psychological Safety

- Managers must commit to recognising and validating the experiences and perspectives of every team member.

- Management behaviours that promote psychological safety include showing vulnerability, practicing inclusivity and demonstrating equitable treatment.

4. Challenges of Establishing Psychological Safety

- Moving from traditional command-and-control leadership paradigms to more inclusive and empathetic approaches is necessary.

- This shift enhances individual and team performance and aligns with modern workforce expectations.

5. SCARF Model

- The SCARF model identifies five social domains influencing behaviour: Status, Certainty, Autonomy, Relatedness and Fairness.

- Managers can use the SCARF model to foster a more engaging and productive work environment.

6. Impact of Leadership Styles on SCARF Domains

- Traditional hierarchical leadership can undermine SCARF principles, leading to reduced autonomy, status and certainty among team members.

- Inclusive and empowering leadership enhances SCARF domains, fostering innovation, engagement and loyalty.

7. **Growth Mindset and Psychological Safety**

- Adopting a growth mindset encourages viewing talents and abilities as improvable through effort and learning from failures.

- Managers should model resilience, promote lifelong learning and normalise failure to foster a growth-oriented and psychologically safe workplace.

8. **Strategies for Cultivating a Growth-Oriented Workplace**

- Model and encourage resilience.

- Promote continuous education and skill development.

- Normalise failure as part of the learning process.

- Celebrate effort and incremental progress.

9. **Integrating Growth Mindset with Psychological Safety**

- Combining a growth mindset with psychological safety creates an environment where team members feel secure to innovate and take on new challenges.

- This approach ensures employees are willing and eager to stretch their capabilities and contribute to their fullest potential.

Reflection Questions

- How can you develop a growth mindset in yourself and others?

- How can you make your team members feel safer at work?

EMPOWERMENT

The beauty of empowering others is that your own
power is not diminished in the process.

—Barbara Coloroso

Empowerment

Empowerment is at the heart of the manager's toolkit and is a multifaceted approach that aims to unlock potential in teams based on their level of skill and motivation. It is the process that helps team members find autonomy to make decisions that can contribute to the success of the organisation. There are five key approaches to empowerment that leaders can adopt: directing (or teaching), delegating, motivating, coaching and holding difficult or tough conversations.

However, it is not just the choice of empowerment strategy that we employ, but the way that we empower that will fundamentally decide whether we are taking the leadership route. Managers need to be aware of SCARF even while empowering others. At Mango Bank, the approaches of Kelly and Sofia vary widely. Through their stories, we will learn how empowerment can transform an organisation or stunt its growth. Empowerment in itself is not enough to lift others unless the intent behind it is to truly help them grow. Many managers may empower others ineffectively, consciously or unconsciously influencing their chances of success.

KELLY

Kelly's approach to empowerment is a bit like a one-size-fits-all sweater. It's functional but not always flattering. Kelly delegates tasks based on what needs to be done and her intent is always efficiency and control. She rarely thinks about whether a task or project fits the skill or interests of her team. When she directs, Kelly's instructions are short and sharp and her expectation is that when she shares her expertise, you need to be paying close attention. Kelly's assumption is that once you have been told – you need to perform. She rarely asks if people are okay to take on a task – after all, she isn't running a charity! Furthermore, she rarely gives praise and when she does, it's for a completed task or a finished project. Hovering around on the office floor, team members might often whisper, 'Kelly is watching' – an alarm that says you need to look busy (even if it's your lunch break). For team members who can't perform, Kelly is on standby with a list of their perceived misdemeanours meticulously written down and logged. When it comes to coaching, Kelly sees this as an exclusive opportunity for her team to receive her select downloads – a bit like being invited to a premiere of a new movie where the spoilers are insights into Kelly's expertise.

Sofia

Close to her team, Sofia is able to develop customised empowerment strategies for each team member. She knows their strengths, interests and level of motivation. For each team member, she employs what she feels is the right empowerment strategy, mindful that her team feels safe and heard in every context. When she directs, Sofia ensures that her team can connect tasks to the bigger picture and that team members feel involved and included. Delegation conversations are an opportunity to check in with her team and make them feel valued and aligned with business strategy. When she needs to motivate team members, Sofia is on hand with carefully phrased words and the right level of push. Always aware of the energy in her office and her team, Sofia doesn't shy away from difficult conversations. Instead, she prepares herself and sets out to understand the reason that performance has dropped – always giving her team members a fair hearing. Lastly, Sofia coaches talent who she feels have more complex challenges to overcome. Her coaching conversations are empathetic and often filled with silence and pauses as she helps her coachees reflect.

Choosing Strategies

The difference between Kelly's and Sofia's approaches highlights the importance of observational skills and knowing your people. Kelly's approach is more functional, and she empowers but always with the end goal of control. With managers, poorly executed empowerment often manifests as giving unclear instructions and, at worst, setting up people to fail. This often helps the manager reinforce their superiority and maintain control as the expert of the task. Of course, organisational culture will reinforce this, and managers may often look up to higher levels of management for their cues. When we follow the leadership route and lead by lifting, we attempt to influence organisational change from within our team first – modelling effective behaviours. By focusing on our own team, we can impact the culture of the entire organisation.

Sofia's approach is more focused on empowering based on her close observations of her team members. This means that she knows who to direct, delegate, motivate, coach and have tough conversations with based on her understanding of her team. Ultimately, her goal is to help her team grow. Sofia is also mindful of SCARF and understands the core social domains that influence motivation and engagement. Moreover, Sofia is motivated by helping to lift her team rather than control them. Thus, her intent is never to sabotage or inhibit team members for fear of them surpassing her.

Empowerment, therefore, is about choosing the right approach for the right individuals. We can map motivation against skill to help us employ the right approach to empowerment. Skill here means the ability to complete a task: like writing a root cause analysis report or solving customer problems in timed conditions.

The matrix in Figure 4 illustrates how the motivation vs skill matrix looks.

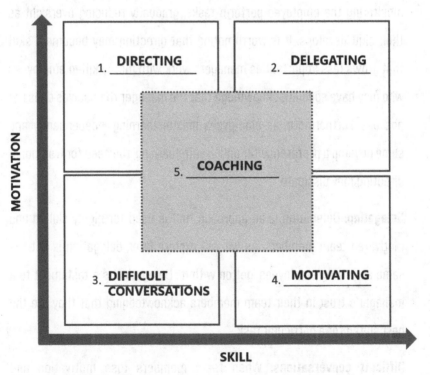

Figure 4: Motivation vs skill

This idea draws from situational leadership and the work of Paul Hershey and Ken Blanchard in the 1960s.[1] It is sometimes referred to as the skill/will matrix and if you do a Google search you will find different versions of the matrix. You probably won't find one like this though.

Let us have a look at each of the five steps to understand the model.

Directing: Directing is really another word for teaching. This involves knowledge transfer to team members who are motivated but lack the skill for the task. Directing involves the manager teaching the skill and then monitoring the employee perform tasks, gradually reducing oversight as their skill develops. It is worth noting that directing may become a skill that grows less important as managers work with more skilled employees who may have specialist knowledge that the manager themselves does not possess. Furthermore, as employees master learning independently and some develop a preference for online self-learning, the need for traditional directing may dissipate.

Delegating: Delegation is an approach that is used for highly skilled and motivated team members. As we will explore later, delegation is not the same as letting employees 'get on with it'. Delegation is a testament to a manager's trust in their team members acknowledging that they are the best suited for a particular task.

Difficult conversations: When team members lose motivation and become unskilled at a task, a difficult conversation is needed. Many managers dread these conversations as they fear breaking relatedness with their team. However, difficult conversations are really open, honest and sometimes challenging discussions that tackle performance issues and set a road map for further development. If they are done well, difficult conversations can be transformative and inspirational, helping poor performers back on the path to successful team contribution.

Motivating: Sometimes skilled employees become demotivated. They may become bored by a task they are good at, or they may feel isolated and lack the feedback they need from managers. As such, motivation is really about feedback. Letting people know how they are doing or that they are valued helps them get back on track.

Coaching: Coaching is the fifth style of empowerment. The fifth element. As such it fits awkwardly into the matrix. The key difference is that coaching involves complex problems that may be affecting performance or an individual reaching their potential. It is a slow approach and requires managers to help coachees find their own solutions. There may be many reasons why we would choose coaching over another empowerment style. Importantly, coaching should not be used exclusively for knowledge transfer as directing is faster and more practical. In addition, coaching should not be used for delegating or motivating unless obstacles emerge that are complex and inhibit an employee's ability to complete a task. In this situation, a manager *might* hold a coaching conversation. Coaching techniques are unlikely to be used in a difficult conversation by a manager as the situation requires a more assertive approach. Nevertheless, coaching conversations might include discussions on strategies to self-motivate as well as more 'difficult' conversations that might attempt to shift a coachee's perspective. The key difference then would be that coaching is all about helping the coachee (the manager's team member) find their own solutions.

Horses for Courses

There is a Japanese saying: 'Junin Toiro', which translates as ten people, ten colours. As people are different, they need different empowerment approaches. In empowerment, we can think of five colours. Essentially, managers need to use the right approach for their people, driven by the right intentions, which in turn are driven by the right beliefs. The following chapters of this book are all about how to use these five styles or colours of empowerment. We will look at each approach and relate it to the foundational ideas we have discussed in Chapters 1 and 2.

Chapter Echo

Rupert Wong's phone call is from one of his people leaders, Cynthia. 'Hi Rupert . . . I need your advice', she says. 'We need to fill the MD Role and have shortlisted two candidates'.

'Go on . . .' says Rupert.

'Well . . . we only had six applications. And we shortlisted two. Eh . . . Kelly from Operations and Sofia . . . from Retail'.

A wry smile crosses Rupert's face.

Key Takeaways – Chapter Three

1. Understanding Empowerment

- Empowerment is about providing employees with autonomy, resources and support to make decisions and contribute meaningfully to the organisation's goals.

- It involves creating an environment where employees feel valued, capable and motivated.

2. Five Key Approaches to Empowerment

- **Delegating:** Entrusting significant responsibilities to highly skilled and motivated employees to foster autonomy and trust.

- **Motivating:** Reigniting drive and engagement in skilled but demotivated employees by aligning tasks with their interests and recognising achievements.

- **Managing difficult conversations:** Addressing performance issues in employees with low skill and motivation through honest, supportive and clear discussions.

- **Directing:** Providing clear instructions and guidance to motivated but less skilled employees, gradually reducing oversight as they develop competence.

- **Coaching:** Guiding all employees through their professional development journey, setting goals, offering feedback and providing necessary resources and support.

3. Impact of Observational Skills

- Effective empowerment requires leaders to understand deeply their team members to choose the right empowerment approach for each individual.

- Observational skills enable leaders to maximise team potential and contribute to professional development.

4. Tailoring Empowerment Strategies

- Delegating for highly skilled and motivated employees to foster trust and autonomy.

- Motivating for skilled but demotivated employees to reignite their passion for work.

- Directing for motivated but less skilled employees to provide clear guidance and build confidence.

- Coaching for helping overcome obstacles to performance and potential.

- Managing difficult conversations with honesty and empathy to address low skill and motivation issues.

Reflection Questions

- How do you decide which approach to use to empower others?

- Why do you think some managers are reluctant to empower others?

DIRECTING

Tell me and I forget, teach me and I may remember,

involve me and I understand.

—Xunxi

REFLECTION TASK: DIRECTING

Instructions: Rate each statement on a scale from Strongly Disagree (1) to Strongly Agree (5).

Statement	Strongly Disagree (1)	Disagree (2)	Neutral (3)	Agree (4)	Strongly Agree (5)
1. I provide detailed explanations of tasks and expectations to my team.					
2. I give quick instructions and expect immediate understanding from my team.					
3. I tailor my instructions to the individual learning needs of each team member.					
4. I expect team members to execute tasks perfectly on their first attempt.					
5. I simplify complex ideas and ensure my team understands them before proceeding.					

Statement	Strongly Disagree (1)	Disagree (2)	Neutral (3)	Agree (4)	Strongly Agree (5)
6. I avoid giving tasks that might lead to failure to maintain a positive image.					
7. I observe and consider the unique strengths and weaknesses of my team members when assigning tasks.					
8. I assume that a single training session is enough for employees to master new skills.					
9. I provide ongoing practice opportunities and constructive feedback to help my team improve.					
10. I mainly focus on giving instructions rather than supporting and guiding my team.					

Read the chapter before you check your answers on p. 261

Managers as Teachers

I remember hearing the saying, 'those who can do, those who can't, teach' in my early years as a teacher and trainer. I always felt it undervalued the importance of teaching and its validity as a skill in its own right. Having spent nearly 20 years in education, I have realised that, first, we all need to teach in life, and secondly, some people are more skilled than others.

Managers need to be able to direct or teach effectively. In doing so, they can speed up the efficiency of knowledge transfer and minimise errors. The better they teach, the faster their team will be able to perform a task. Effective directing relies on a manager's ability to explain complex ideas and present them in a way that connects with their audience's level of knowledge and learning preferences.

Unfortunately, many managers expect that a single 'lesson' is enough for a team member to achieve mastery of a skill. A bit like a teacher expecting a student to hold a conversation in basic Vietnamese after one conversation class. Managers must understand that employees might not grasp new concepts or tasks immediately and be able to execute them straight away.

Managers should also be aware of the levels of learning that are required to complete a task. Some tasks may require memorisation whilst others may require more critical thinking skills. I often hear managers complaining that their team never 'question the status quo' or critically evaluate things. This may often be as they have not been taught to do this.

An important lesson about teaching can be taken from Japanese folklore and the story of Urashima Taro, a fisherman.[1] One day, in an act of kindness, he saves a turtle from being bullied by a group of children. The turtle is so grateful that he rewards Taro by taking him to the Dragon Palace under the sea to meet the beautiful princess Otohime. After being treated like a king for what seems like several days, Taro eventually wants to go home. Before he leaves, and as a gift, the princess gives him a box called the Tamatebako. The princess tells him to keep the box with him – but never open it. When Taro returns home, he realises that what seemed like a few days in the Dragon Palace was actually hundreds of years in his own world. Confused and saddened that everything he knew has gone, Taro decides to open the box. Instantly, he is transformed into an old man. The Tamatebako had contained his lost years!

The story serves as a powerful reminder to managers that simply giving instructions without the 'why' behind them can have negative consequences. Furthermore, connecting directives to the bigger picture helps managers make their team feel included and elevates their *status*. A hospital cleaner, for example, needs to know how their work is essential to the bigger picture to feel engaged.

In this chapter, we will return briefly to the stories of Kelly and Sofia, before exploring two key theories that might help you understand the most effective ways to give directives.

KELLY

In her haste to get things done, Kelly often rushes through instructions, following things up with a brusque 'do you understand?' This approach, whilst seeming efficient, often puts her team on the spot. Fearing that they might seem incompetent or downright stupid, many of her team nod in agreement, even though they are unclear about the task.

Take Siva's story as a case in point. When Kelly gave him a hurried overview of a new software the bank was using, she followed up with a quick 'got it?'. Siva, feeling under pressure to not seem inadequate, nodded, despite a deep sense of unease in the pit of his stomach. This lack of clarity ended up with a significant error in processing a key client transaction, causing embarrassment for the team and denting Mango Bank's reputation.

When giving directions, Kelly likes to download. Rushing through the steps of a process and rarely monitoring her team perform the task. Her expectation is that one of Kelly's famous lessons is enough for knowledge transfer and for her team to be able to apply whatever task she has taught.

Sofia

Sofia gives directives with SCARF in mind. Her aim is never to sabotage or emphasise her superiority. She begins explaining any task with a clear link to its 'why' and the bigger team or organisational picture. This helps her team connect the task to team goals and the customers. This bigger picture vision adds value to tasks and helps her team connect more operational tasks to the human element (a bit like our janitor putting a man on the moon!). She also appreciates that learning takes time and modifies her directive style based on her team member's level of competence. As time passes and team members develop competence, Sofia reduces her level of monitoring, pushing her team to become more and more self-sufficient. She also remembers that her best teachers at school were the ones who tried to get their students to *apply* learning rather than simply remember. Sofia remembers Mr Gopi and his famous chemistry classes, where his students would end up singeing their hair on the Bunsen burners whilst intensely learning about the properties of magnesium! Finally, Sofia always makes people feel like she is prepared to make time for them. Nothing is rushed and she often asks team members to paraphrase a task to ensure comprehension. This allows her team to internalise anything she has directed and demonstrate comprehension by using their own words.

Two Teachers

Both managers are teachers. Kelly presents the traditional role of the teacher as an expert – a bit like lecturers at many universities. She saves time by giving out instructions quickly and expects her team to be constantly focused. However, while she may save time in the short term, Kelly sometimes sows the seeds of longer-term problems where team members make errors due to lack of support. Conversely, Sofia's approach is grounded in providing clarity and certainty. This fosters a learning environment where staff feel supported and competent, which in turn leads to improved performance and fewer mistakes. This story underlines the importance of thoughtful direction and that how we deliver is almost as important as the instructions themselves.

The Competency Ladder

The competency ladder (see Figure 5) is a powerful way to explain how people acquire a skill for a task. Devised by Noel Burch in the 1970s[2] and based on his observations from training and a synthesis of ideas from psychology, the competency ladder explores how learners move from unconscious incompetence to unconscious competence.

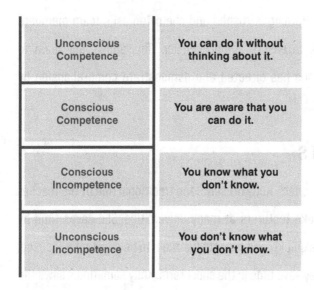

Unconscious Competence	You can do it without thinking about it.
Conscious Competence	You are aware that you can do it.
Conscious Incompetence	You know what you don't know.
Unconscious Incompetence	You don't know what you don't know.

Figure 5: The competency ladder

The idea of competency is easily illustrated through the common experience of learning how to drive. Remember the first time you thought about driving? You probably had no idea about what a blind spot was or how much distance a car needs to come to a stop. You might have thought that parallel parking was easiest if you used the front of the car. There were lots of things that you didn't know you didn't know (unconscious incompetence). Then you attended your driving class and realised there's loads of other stuff you didn't know. This is called conscious incompetence or where you become aware of the things you didn't know. Now whizz forwards several months and you have learned how to drive. You sit behind the wheel upright, hands clenching the steering wheel, strictly following the order in which you learned how to perform the task. Can you remember how stressful it was when you first started? The exhaustion of all that focus. You probably thought to yourself . . . this driving thing really isn't that much fun. Now fast forward again . . . a few more months. Now you can perform the task with minimal effort. You have reached unconscious competence and are relying on your autopilot or System One (automation) as pioneering psychologist Daniel Kahneman might say.[3] You now feel incredibly relaxed, nattering away to your friend in the passenger seat or singing along to your favourite David Bowie song.

Climbing the Ladder

Let's take a look at the competency ladder and explore the lessons we can learn from it about giving effective directions. We will use a conversation between Sofia and her highly talented team member Ken to illustrate how Sofia's awareness of the ladder informs her communication.

Unconscious Incompetence

Ken has been managing projects using his tried-and-tested methods of spreadsheets and email communication. He feels that his methods work and sees no need to use the new software that Mango Bank has introduced. Let's listen in to Sofia's conversation with Ken.

Sofia: Hey Ken, I notice that you have been doing a great job tracking your projects through your spreadsheets. I think our new tool might make your project management even more efficient and collaborative.

Ken: Thanks Sofia . . . I'm happy with my spreadsheets, though. They seem to be working fine for me right now.

Sofia: I get it Ken. But let me give you a quick comparison. Roughly how long do you spend updating spreadsheets and then emailing them to the team?

Ken: I guess an hour or so every day . . .

Sofia: So, with the new software, any updates are tracked automatically. Everyone can see real-time progress without needing to get an email. It has a feature for assigning tasks and deadlines as well as a cool document sharing feature. Imagine cutting that 1 hour into 10 minutes Ken . . . Think of what you could do with your time!

Ken: I didn't realise the software could do all that. I suppose I hadn't really thought about the amount of time I had spent on updates.

Sofia: Exactly. I found that the tool can ramp up my productivity and it's really helped me and the team avoid duplicating tasks. Let's explore the new tool together and see how we can help it benefit you and the team.

Here Sofia highlights the inefficiencies in Ken's current approach and explains the potential benefits of the new software. This awareness is the first step in Ken's journey to mastering the new tool.

Conscious Incompetence

This is a crucial stage where managers need to acknowledge the challenges team members face and offer clear directions. Let's have a look at how Sofia manages the evolving situation.

Ken has accepted that he needs to learn the new software. However, he lacks the necessary skills required to perform the task.

Ken: Okay Sofia, so I can totally see the benefits of the new software. The thing is I'm not familiar with it at all. To be honest, I feel a little bit overwhelmed.

Sofia: I know what you mean, Ken. Learning something new always feels challenging at first. The main thing is that you are open to it and that's a step in the right direction.

Ken: Yeah ... it's just that I'm worried about making mistakes and slowing down the whole team.

Sofia: It's totally normal to feel like that Ken. Remember that we are all learning together. I have arranged for you and some others in the team to do some training with me tomorrow. Don't worry, I will be there to support you after the training too.

Ken: Thanks Sofia . . . that does sound reassuring. So, when do I start the training?

Sofia: I have booked the meeting room for you, Tamar and Jaqueline tomorrow. Level 7. We'll go over the interface and main features and after that I will discuss how to set up a project and team collaboration. How does that sound?

Ken: That sounds good, I guess. I appreciate the support.

Sofia: Remember tomorrow to ask me anything you like! There's no such thing as a silly question and I'm here to help. I will also show you how you can access the online content and user guides on our Learning Management System.

Ken: That will be really helpful. Thanks Sofia!

Sofia: Your welcome Ken! I'm here to help you succeed. Let's do this one step at a time.

We can see that Sofia acknowledges Ken's feelings and provides reassurance and clear expectations. She helps Ken navigate the conscious incompetence stage and avoid feeling overwhelmed. She focuses on providing a supportive environment, which can help encourage growth and development.

CONSCIOUS COMPETENCE

At this stage, individuals have gained the skills and knowledge they need. However, applying these skills requires effort and concentration.

Ken has attended the training sessions and worked through the online content. He is using the new software, but this still requires effort.

KEN: Hi Sofia! I've been using the new software for over a week now and I think I'm starting to get the hang of it! I still find myself double checking things and I think I'm still a bit slow.

SOFIA: That sounds totally normal Ken. I feel like you are making great progress! The fact that you are being so thorough shows that you are committed to doing it right.

KEN: Thanks Sofia . . . I just want to make sure that I don't miss anything important.

SOFIA: I know how you feel Ken. Look, why don't we schedule a meeting later this week. We can go over anything that you are still unsure about. We can look at some of the projects that you have managed to set up so far.

KEN: That would be great Sofia. I'm still a bit unsure about some of the new features so it would be great if we could go over them.

SOFIA: Absolutely, let's do that. Remember that learning something new is a bit like learning to drive. At first, we are very detail-focused but as time passes, we become more natural and fluent . . . a bit like playing a sport.

I remember when I first started rock climbing. It would be intense, and I would really think through every move. I'm no mountain goat now Ken, but I feel more relaxed and natural.

KEN: That makes sense Sofia. I feel I'm getting more fluent, but I still need to think through each step.

SOFIA: You are doing great Ken. Remember my door is always open if you need to ask anything.

Sofia continues to offer support at this stage and reinforce the positive aspects of Ken's learning journey. She makes herself relatable and shares her own learning journey. This helps to prevent Ken from giving up or reverting to his old way of doing things. There is a saying in Malay, 'Genggam bara api biar sampai jadi arang', which translates as 'hold the ember until it becomes ash'. Many of us give up on acquiring a skill or task when the embers are still glowing.

UNCONSCIOUS COMPETENCE

Finally, the skill or task becomes almost automatic, and employees can perform the task effortlessly. At this stage managers can encourage their team to share knowledge of their skills. Furthermore, they can encourage critical thinking and innovation, looking for ways to further enhance the process.

Ken has reached this stage, and the system has become second nature to him. He is now confident in his ability to use the software and feels less cognitive strain whilst performing it.

Sofia: I've noticed that you are using the new tool a lot now Ken . . .

Ken: Yes, it's really helped me speed up managing my projects. My team are much happier too.

Sofia: Great effort Ken!

Ken: Thanks . . . I've even started exploring some of the more advanced features.

Sofia: Great! I'd love to see you share some of this knowledge with others. Perhaps you could run a mini training session or develop a guide?

Ken: I would love to do that. I think I could help get people up to speed more quickly.

Sofia: I think sharing your expertise can help solidify your own knowledge and provide real value to your team. Have you managed to find any new features or workflows that we could benefit from?

Ken: Actually, I have found a few. There are a few automation processes that can save us a bunch of time. Let me put together a presentation on how we can integrate them into our processes. I can then let the team go away and try out the skills. I guess I will need to start by telling the team how these tools can help.

Sofia: That sounds perfect. Let's schedule a meeting where you can share these insights with the team. It's really inspiring to see how you have grown into an expert on the software Ken. I'm really looking forward to seeing how we can continue to innovate as a team.

Ken has reached unconscious competence, and his use of the software is now effortless. Sofia acknowledges this and encourages Ken to share this knowledge with the team. This helps create a motivator for Ken to continue growing and encourages a culture of innovation and growth in the team. Sofia has now lifted Ken through the stages of the competency ladder, and he is now able to analyse the processes, evaluate them and potentially create new ways of using the tool.

By using the competency ladder as a reference, we can enhance the way we give directives. The ladder underscores the need for awareness and preparation before we direct others. Managers must be aware of where their team members stand on the ladder to tailor their approach. This helps to prevent the same rushed instructions we saw Kelly offer to Siva and the resultant mess. Instead, Sofia's approach offers a growth-oriented and supportive environment. She modifies her approach at each stage of the ladder on Ken's learning journey, offering support and encouragement. She also raises awareness of the stages of learning which in turn can help Ken appreciate how he learns and how he can transfer knowledge himself.

A Process for Directives

So, the competency ladder gives us an idea of how people acquire a skill and the approach a manager should take at different stages on the ladder. But what about when we need to actually teach the skill? In the situation described, we didn't get to see how Sofia did this.

When we direct or teach, we should be mindful of SCARF, a model developed by Dr. David Rock and the NeuroLeadership Institute. Can you remember the model we discovered earlier? SCARF stood for Status, Certainty, Awareness, Relatedness and Fairness. We can employ SCARF when we give instructions to generate that more receptive reward state, we discussed in Chapter 2. Let's look at a nine-step approach that managers can use when they provide directives. We will then jump into a conversation that Sofia has with one of her team: Lucy.

STEP ONE: EXPLAIN THE OBJECTIVE OF THE TASK AND ITS BENEFITS (THE WHY)

This stage is where the manager connects the task to the bigger picture and explores its benefits. It is designed for use in the stage of unconscious incompetence where people do not know what they do not know. *A bit like how a fish doesn't know it needs water until someone drains the pond.* This also helps the person receiving the directive have a sense of *certainty* as it increases clarity about the 'why' of the task. Furthermore, it can increase the employee's sense of *status* as they can connect the task to a higher purpose.

STEP TWO: SHOW HOW THE TASK WILL LOOK ON COMPLETION (IF POSSIBLE)

In step two, we try to provide the employee with a visual or descriptive goal to aim for. This stage helps the learner have a clear sense of what they need to achieve. This can help increase *certainty* and reduce any anxiety about expectations. Some managers jump straight into the first step of a task and forget this important stage. It might be a bit like laying the foundations of a building and having no idea of what the building will look like on completion.

STEP THREE: EXPLAIN THE STEPS (THE WHAT)

This is the main part of the directive and the one that most managers are familiar with. Clear steps help ramp up *certainty* as the manager lays out a blueprint for how to complete the task.

STEP FOUR: SHOW HOW TO COMPLETE THE STEPS AND ANY TOOLS (THE HOW)

At this stage the manager creates further *certainty* but also a sense of *autonomy* and empowerment as the employee is shown clearly how they can complete the task.

STEP FIVE: SHOW THE ROLE OF ANYONE ELSE IN THE TASK

In this part of the process, the manager has a chance to connect the task to anyone else involved. This helps address *relatedness* and *fairness* by clarifying everyone's roles and helping to foster a sense of team cohesion and the idea of equitable workload distribution.

STEP SIX: EXPLAIN THE TIMEFRAME OF THE TASK (THE WHEN)

In this stage, the manager sets a clear expectation about the timeline of the task. This also contributes to *certainty* and *autonomy* as team members have a clear idea of the timeframe and some autonomy on how to plan their time.

STEP SEVEN: CHECK/TEST THAT THE PERSON HAS UNDERSTOOD

At this stage, the manager attempts to check for comprehension. Apart from asking for questions, this can be done by asking the team member to paraphrase the task or by asking questions that sensitively check comprehension . The manager should avoid asking: 'do you understand?' in case they trigger the employee feeling threatened. Instead, managers can ask questions like 'how would you explain this to someone else in the team?', which allow the team member to paraphrase the task by taking on the role of teacher themselves. By carefully checking for comprehension, the manager helps increase *certainty* by verifying understanding and even addresses *status* by involving the employee in the conversation, valuing their input and comprehension.

Step Eight: Monitor the Person Doing the Task

Here the manager monitors the person doing the task. This should try to resemble support as closely as possible without the manager micromanaging or belittling the employee in any way. Managers should schedule regular check-ins to ensure that the other person can ask for guidance and make any adjustments. This approach helps the manager maintain a sense of *autonomy* and *relatedness*.

Step Nine: Providing Feedback

This is the final stage where the manager provides positive reinforcements and asks the employee suggestions for further improvement. If this is done correctly, the manager can help address the domains of *status, relatedness* and *fairness*. All of these can help the team member feel enriched by the learning process and further engaged.

By weaving the SCARF model into how we give directives, we help guide the effective transmission of knowledge and skills whilst supporting a nurturing and positive work environment. This helps transform directives from simply being commands to opportunities for growth, learning and meaningful contribution. Let's listen to Sofia follow this nine-step model (see Figure 6) in her discussion with her direct report, Lucy. She is showing Lucy how to use the software to enhance project management.

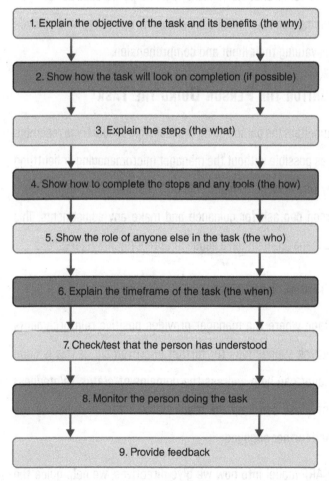

1. Explain the objective of the task and its benefits (the why)

2. Show how the task will look on completion (if possible)

3. Explain the steps (the what)

4. Show how to complete the steps and any tools (the how)

5. Show the role of anyone else in the task (the who)

6. Explain the timeframe of the task (the when)

7. Check/test that the person has understood

8. Monitor the person doing the task

9. Provide feedback

Figure 6: Directives Process Flow

Sofia and Lucy

STEP ONE: EXPLAIN THE OBJECTIVE OF THE TASK AND ITS BENEFITS (THE WHY)

Sofia: Hi Lucy, can I talk to you about a new task that is essential for our upcoming project?

Lucy: Yep, sure Sofia.

Sofia: Well, we need to implement a new project management tool to streamline our workflow and improve team collaboration. The software is a real game changer and will help us speed up our productivity, avoid duplication of work and reduce errors.

Lucy: That sounds interesting Sofia. How does it connect to our current workflow?

Sofia: Great question! Well, the software will integrate with our current tools. It is designed to make our lives easier.

STEP TWO: SHOW HOW THE TASK WILL LOOK ON COMPLETION (IF POSSIBLE)

Sofia: Let me show you an example of a completed project that we designed using this software (opening her laptop). Here's a demo version that shows you how tasks are organised, deadlines are set, and progress is tracked. You can see the details at a glance, which is a really cool feature.

Lucy: That looks really organised Sofia.

Sofia: Exactly. I think this will definitely improve our coordination.

Step Three: Explain the Steps (The What)

Sofia: Okay. Now let's go through the steps to set up a new project using the tool. First of all, we need to create a project outline. After that, you'll add tasks and assign them to the different team members. After that, we'll learn how to set deadlines and milestones. Finally, we will explore the tracking tool so that we can monitor task progress.

Lucy: That sounds very manageable.

Step Four: Show How to Complete the Steps and Any Tools (The How)

Sofia: Let me show you how to complete each step. Let's start off by making a project outline. (Sofia proceeds to demonstrate each step.)

Lucy: It really helps for me to see each step.

Step Five: Show the Role of Anyone Else in the Task (The Who)

Sofia: For this task you will be collaborating with Shelfia at the start as she is familiar with our current workflows. After that, everyone will be responsible for their own tasks, and you will be overseeing the overall progress and making sure people stay on track.

Lucy: So, I will coordinate with Shelfia first and then manage the team's progress using the new tool.

Step Six: Explain the Timeframe of the Task (The When)

Sofia: We want to start using the new tool for our big project. So, we have about two weeks to get things set up. This will also give us time to iron out any possible issues.

Step Seven: Check/Test That the Person Has Understood

Sofia: So, Lucy, are you confident with the steps of the process? Do you have any questions or concerns at this stage?

Lucy: I think I've got it. I might need some help with the setup, though.

Sofia: No problem. I'm here to help you when you need it.

Step Eight: Monitor the Person Doing the Task

Sofia: I'll check in with you regularly to monitor your progress. We can have daily stand-up discussions to address any challenges you are facing. I'm here to support you, Lucy.

... After some time

Step Nine: Provide Feedback

Sofia: Your progress so far has been great. How are things going with Shelfia?

Lucy: Things are going great . . . I think I may have found a way we can speed things up even more.

Sofia: (smiling) Go on . . . .

Bloom's Taxonomy

There is one more learning model that is useful as a reference for managers giving directives. That is Bloom's Taxonomy (see Figure 7). Benjamin Bloom was an educational psychologist who in the 1950s came up with a hierarchy of learning objectives.[4] The hierarchy was based on the level of complexity for the way people learn and serves as a powerful insight into how people think. Managers can leverage the taxonomy to help their team perform a task and go beyond application.

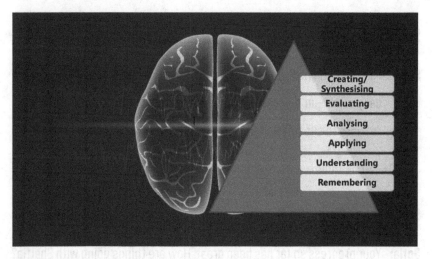

Figure 7: Bloom's Taxonomy

Team members who are simply encouraged to stay business as usual (BAU) focused are likely to do just that. Managers need to encourage analysis, evaluation and synthesis to really help disrupt the business and generate new ideas.

REMEMBER AND UNDERSTAND

At these foundational levels, the focus is on recalling information and being able to process it. Managers should ensure that team members have a solid understanding of the required knowledge before making tasks more complex.

It is crucial for managers to realise that remembering information is not the same as understanding it. This may be particularly relevant for team members who have come from a background with a focus on rote learning and memory recall.

For instance, employees may be able to list the company values from a handbook or from posters in the office. This is an act of recall (the remember level of the taxonomy) and does not signify that they grasp the deeper meaning of these values or how they should influence decision-making or behaviour. This disconnect often means that staff members are unable to relate to the corporate jargon a company may have spent millions finetuning. Understanding, the higher level of the taxonomy, will involve unpacking these values. Managers can ask employees to paraphrase instructions to ensure that they have understood them. In some cases, managers might ask team members to translate instructions into their own language.

ANALYSE

Analysis involves breaking down information into its different parts to help understand its structure and how the different parts relate. Managers can encourage analysis by asking their team members to examine systems, tasks or projects critically. By breaking down tasks into parts, team members might be able to identify areas for improvement.

EVALUATE

Evaluation is really about making a judgement on the information that is presented. This might involve evaluating proposals or data presentations. Managers should encourage capable team members to evaluate the outcomes of projects and decision-making. By soliciting their perspective, they can keep their team engaged and enhance their critical thinking. Managers who encourage evaluation should be ready for debates and pushback on their own ideas. This will be difficult for more controlling managers like Kelly to handle as they might be threatened by what they perceive as a personal attack.

CREATE

The final level of Bloom's Taxonomy involves putting things together to form a new whole. This is the idea of synthesis and often the most disruptive ideas come from this top level of the hierarchy. Managers can help their team create or synthesise by giving them time to do so. They can also help their team be creative by exposing them to different parts of the business, different processes and products and even different industries. But more on this later.

PUTTING IT ALL TOGETHER

Managers can use these models to improve how they give their directives. This must start with empathy and many managers cling to old models of how people learn as this is what they went through themselves at school or university or even with their own managers. By thinking of the competence ladder, managers can slowly increase the autonomy of team members. They must remember that fluency in a task takes time.

Secondly, they can remember Bloom's Taxonomy to guide their team toward higher levels of thinking. I call this *thought leading*. This differs from the standard definition of thought leading which is about positioning yourself as an expert. Rather managers can model critical and creative thinking to their teams and encourage them to challenge the tried and tested way of doing things.

But remember, if your managerial modus operandi is control, you are unlikely to get innovation and creativity. If people aspire to perfection, why would they make mistakes? Nevertheless, we should remember that we wouldn't have penicillin without trial and error or . . . Post-it notes™. So, take a Post-it right now, stick it on your laptop and write a reminder to yourself of the importance of mistakes.

Chapter Echo

Rupert's conversation with Cynthia had got him thinking. What makes a great manager? He takes a bite into the still warm steamed bun that his wife had passed him for lunch. The rich taste of the salted egg yolk suddenly transports him back to high school – St Josephs.

His mind flits back to his school days and pauses at his history teacher: Mrs Kwan. Ahh Mrs Kwan … she was different from his other teachers who would lecture and coerce their students to memorise facts and events. Mrs Kwan's classroom was always noisy, a real hubbub of activity. It was the sound of people learning, he reflects. Once when Mrs Kwan asked the class to reenact a historical event, Rupert and his classmates had been reserved. 'Why can't we just read about it in the books, Mrs Kwan?' a cheekier student Vincent had asked. Mrs Kwan had replied that the best way to learn 'is by doing. We need to live it to feel it'.

Brushing the crumbs off his Brioni suit, Rupert takes a sip of his now cold green tea. Perhaps the managers of the future are more like teachers, he thinks. 'Dong', the sound of the intercom interrupts his thoughts …

Key Takeaways: Chapter Four

1. Effective Directing

- Directing closely resembles teaching and involves transferring knowledge, skills and expectations from the manager to the employee.
- Good directing requires clear communication, patience, understanding of diverse learning needs and continuous support.

- Managers should articulate tasks and goals clearly, help employees understand the significance and methodology of their tasks and create a supportive atmosphere for learning and improvement.

2. Contrasting Management Styles

- Managers rushing through instructions may lead to confusion and mistakes, often resulting in mismatched tasks and employee capabilities.

- Providing clear, detailed instructions and support fosters an environment where employees feel secure and capable. Tailoring the approach to individual needs and encouraging continuous learning is more effective.

3. Competency Ladder

- **Unconscious incompetence:** Employees are unaware of what they don't know. Managers need to raise awareness and highlight the necessity of new skills.

- **Conscious incompetence:** Employees recognise their knowledge gaps. Managers should provide encouragement, training and clear steps for learning.

- **Conscious competence:** Employees gain skills but require effort and concentration to apply them. Managers should recognise progress and provide ongoing support and feedback.

- **Unconscious competence:** Employees perform tasks effortlessly. Managers should maintain and further develop skills, encouraging innovation and knowledge sharing.

4. Process Approach for Giving Directives

- **Explain the objective:** Clarify the importance and benefits of the task (Why).

- **Show completion example:** Provide a visual or descriptive goal (What).

- **Explain steps:** Detail the specific actions needed (What).

- **Show how to complete steps:** Demonstrate the application of skills (How).

- **Show role of others:** Clarify everyone's roles (Who).

- **Explain timeframe:** Set clear deadlines (When).

- **Check understanding:** Verify comprehension and address questions.

- **Monitor progress:** Provide guidance and adjustments as needed.

- **Provide feedback:** Recognise achievements and offer constructive feedback.

5. SCARF Model Integration

- Ensures that directives align with employees' psychological needs: Status, Certainty, Autonomy, Relatedness and Fairness.

- Creates a supportive, engaging and psychologically safe work environment.

6. Bloom's Taxonomy in Management

- **Remember and understand:** Ensure a solid grasp of knowledge before moving to complex tasks.

- **Apply:** Encourage practical application of learned skills.

- **Analyse:** Foster critical examination of tasks and projects.

- **Evaluate:** Involve team members in decision-making and evaluating outcomes.

- **Create:** Challenge team members to innovate and develop new solutions.

By incorporating these takeaways, managers can enhance their empowerment strategies, leading to more effective, motivated and cohesive teams.

Reflection Questions

- How can we encourage others to think critically?

- How can managers encourage others to challenge them?

DELEGATING

If you are the smartest person in the room, then you are in the wrong room.

—Source Unknown

REFLECTION TASK: DELEGATION

Instructions: Rate each statement on a scale from Strongly Disagree (1) to Strongly Agree (5).

Statement	Strongly Disagree (1)	Disagree (2)	Neutral (3)	Agree (4)	Strongly Agree (5)
1. I clearly outline the goals and expectations of the task before delegating.					
2. I assign tasks without providing detailed instructions or necessary resources.					
3. I maintain regular check-ins to offer support and ensure progress.					
4. I assume capable team members do not need follow-up or support once a task is delegated.					
5. I provide examples and resources to help the team member understand the task better.					
6. I delegate tasks without explaining their purpose or importance.					

Statement	Strongly Disagree (1)	Disagree (2)	Neutral (3)	Agree (4)	Strongly Agree (5)
7. I offer assistance and make it clear that I am available to help if needed.					
8. I expect team members to handle tasks independently without any check-ins.					
9. I express trust and confidence in the team member's abilities to complete the task.					
10. I delegate tasks to team members who lack the skills or resources to complete them.					
11. I ensure the team member understands the task by asking them to summarise their understanding.					
12. I take over tasks that were delegated if progress is not immediately visible.					

Read the chapter before you check your answers on p. 262

The Importance of Delegation

If we remember the skill vs motivation matrix, delegating was the approach for both skilled and motivated team members. These are craftspeople – masters of their art, often more skilled than the managers themselves. Picture a team like risk and data analytics in Mango Bank. In this team a manager might have experts who do anything from developing complex risk models to keeping up with regulatory changes, using breakthrough technology for data analytics. A manager may or may not possess these skills.

Or let's think of a kitchen in a world-class Thai restaurant. A bit yummier than data analytics! In that kitchen, sweltering under the heat of grills, huge pans and plumes of steam, you would have a team with incredible expertise. An executive chef, head chef, sous chef, chef de partie, commis chef, sauce chef and pastry chef, each with specialist skills. While the executive chef may not be able to make a Tom Yam as effectively as the chef de partie, he will know what a good Tom Yam tastes like: creamy, the right balance of spiciness and sourness and sweetness with a touch of umami.

In the same way, a manager might not have the skillset of a certain team member but should be able to evaluate the result of a piece of work or project.

When I ask managers what delegation is, their answer is often something like 'letting people get on with it' or being laissez-faire. However, impactful delegation is far more nuanced than simply assigning a task and stepping away. It involves setting clear goals, ensuring the necessary resources as well as conducting regular check-ins to evaluate progress and potentially help remove obstacles.

Setting goals at the start of a delegating conversation is of course paramount to success. This might mean stipulating the standard to define success and key information like the timeline. Without clearly defined goals, even the most motivated team member can struggle to meet expectations. This in turn might affect their morale and cause them to slip into the demotivated box in the matrix.

Regular check-ins are also a fundamental part of delegation. These are not meant to micromanage team members but rather to offer support, feedback and adjustments to the task if necessary. It also signals to the employee that they are not alone in their efforts and that the manager remains a support system and resource who can help them when needed.

This approach to delegation strikes a balance between autonomy and support, with the manager able to provide direction and ensure alignment with broader organisational objectives. It is a dynamic process that should foster individual growth and in turn outstanding organisational results.

As you can probably guess, Kelly and Sofia take a very different approach to delegation.

KELLY

In Operations at Mango Bank, Kelly treats delegation as a way of being hands off with her team. Let's take the example of Wei Min, one of Kelly's prize assets and a genuine expert in the division. We see Kelly, keen to offload a task, deciding to offload an important client report to Wei Min. With a pinch of nervousness, he accepts, eager to showcase his abilities to Kelly.

Kelly's instructions are brief and hurried, a bit like a note left stuck to the fridge to remind you to buy some more fish sauce or food for the cat. 'Ensure the report is comprehensive and I will need it by next Wednesday' instructs Kelly as she pirouettes quickly into the next meeting.

Wei Min, well renowned for his ability to distil information into concise and readable reports, gets started. He draws on his experience for other big Mango Bank clients and creates a mosaic of text and powerful data visualisation to impress the client. Wei Min ensures that his report is readable for lay people and simplifies the more complex technical information for non-experts. He spends half of his Saturday finetuning the report, and finally late Tuesday sits back in his chair to admire his masterpiece.

Wednesday morning, Wei Min pings the email attachment to Kelly. Within seconds, a reply appears in his inbox with the brusque response: 'Noted'.

Fast forward to Wednesday afternoon and Kelly summons Wei Min into her office. Her disappointment is palpable. What transpires is that Kelly expected the report to be readable for a very specific audience, familiar with the more technical language and requiring a deeper dive into the issues concerned. Wei Min, more used to writing reports that circulate to a broader and more generalist readership, feels unjustly criticised. He had been given the task without any clear guidance on how he could excel. Wei Min began to question Kelly's intentions – sabotage?

Kelly, clearly showing her disdain, launches into a lecture on the importance of attention to detail and high standards. Wei Min, crestfallen, makes a mental note to request his holiday leave earlier than anticipated.

The incident becomes an unintentional story that illustrates a missed opportunity for effective delegation and mentorship. For Kelly, however, it serves to reinforce her mental superiority over her team and her timeless adage of doing things herself. It is the reminder that she needs to oversee tasks more directly to succeed. Conversely, Wei Min has become demotivated, questioning his own ability and developing a resentment of Kelly based on what he perceives as a lack of fairness.

Sofia

Sofia's approach at Mango Bank contrasts sharply with Kelly's. The story of Sofia and Sebastien, a talented but under-the-radar team member, illustrates this perfectly.

Sofia begins by sitting down with Sebastien and explaining her reasons for delegating the work to him. Kelly states her trust in Sebastien being able to perform the task effectively. She goes on to provide him with a comprehensive overview of the project, outlining the goals as well as the expectations. She also connects the project to the bank's overall strategy. Unlike Kelly's cryptic commands, Sofia provides a clear road map, offering Sebastien certainty. Sofia couples this with invitations for questions and carefully worded ways of checking for comprehension. She also shares resources and examples of similar successful projects, thus ensuring that Sebastien has a solid foundation on which to build.

Throughout the project, Sofia maintains a clear line of communication, never micromanaging but offering support and guidance. She checks in regularly to offer feedback and encouragement while ensuring the project is still aligned with its objectives.

As the project nears completion, it becomes clear that Sebastien has exceeded expectations. When Sebastien presents the project to senior leaders in Mango Bank, Sofia steps back, allowing Sebastien to bask in the praise for his hard work.

Behind the scenes, Sofia's approach has fostered a great sense of loyalty in Sebastien, who feels supported and valued. This sense of engagement helps Sebastien develop his confidence and he feels ready to experiment with tasks and challenge himself even further.

A Process Approach

Do you remember Dr David Rock and the Neuroleadership Institute's SCARF model? That's Status, Certainty, Autonomy, Relatedness and Fairness. We can utilise SCARF, as we did with giving directives, to make delegation effective (see Figure 8) and ensure that our conversations are inspiring. Let's take a look at a step-by-step guide and then we will watch Sofia in action by rewinding her first discussion with Sebastien.

STEP ONE: MENTION WHY YOU ARE DELEGATING TO THIS PERSON

In this step, the manager has the chance to make the team member feel valued and in turn raise their sense of *status*. We might acknowledge their previous efforts and contributions and state that we have trust in their ability to complete the project or task.

STEP TWO: TALK ABOUT THE PURPOSE OF THE TASK

In this step, the manager has the chance to reduce ambiguity and help the team member understand the bigger picture. This can enhance *certainty* by helping the team member envisage the end goal and increase *status* by making them feel the task is valuable.

STEP THREE: MENTION WHY THE TASK IS IMPORTANT AND THE CONSEQUENCES OF IT BEING INCOMPLETE OR NOT UP TO STANDARD

Here the manager can establish the impact of the task, which can help the respondent sense its importance and increase their perception of *status*. It also serves as an opportunity to reinforce the impact of it not being done effectively.

STEP FOUR: EXPLAIN THE TIMEFRAME

Next, the manager can establish a clear timeline, which can help offer a sense of structure and predictability and further enhance *certainty*.

STEP FIVE: TALK ABOUT ACTIONS WHICH NEED TO BE COMPLETED

This step is where the manager spells out the key details of the task and makes it clear that the team member can complete the task in the way which they know best. This further helps to increase *certainty* as well as *autonomy*, as the team member feels they have freedom to complete the task in the way that they know best.

STEP SIX: MENTION THE STANDARD OF THE ACTIONS WHICH NEED TO BE COMPLETED

The manager here sets expectations for the quality of work and makes sure that the team member comprehends these standards. This helps the manager increase *certainty* and a sense of *fairness* in their task by explaining the objective measures by which success will be measured.

STEP SEVEN: OFFER ANY ASSISTANCE

By offering support, the manager helps increase a sense of *relatedness*. The manager would reinforce that they or the team are available and willing to help which can help foster an environment of collaboration.

Step Eight: Mention That You Have Trust and Confidence in the Other Person

By expressing trust and confidence in the team member, the manager reinforces their sense of *status* and *autonomy* as they encourage them to take full ownership of the task.

Step Nine: Check for Understanding

Here the manager would check for understanding by asking any questions. This further ramps up *certainty*.

Step Ten: Ask the Person to Summarise or Paraphrase What They Have to Do

This gives the manager the chance to further ensure understanding and increase *certainty*. If we remember Bloom's Taxonomy, this shows that the team member has internalised and understood the instructions. However, it is important that the manager does not sound patronising in how they frame this.

Step Eleven: Ask the Other Person if They Have Any Questions

This allows the other person the opportunity to ask any questions and can further increase certainty.

STEP TWELVE: CONFIRM THAT THEY CAN AND WILL DO THE TASK

In this final confirmation, the manager provides an opportunity for the individual to commit to the task, reinforcing a sense of *autonomy* and empowerment. What if they say 'no' at this stage I hear you ask? They won't.

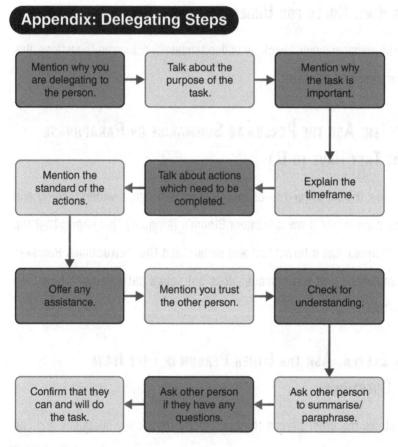

Appendix: Delegating Steps

Mention why you are delegating to the person. → Talk about the purpose of the task. → Mention why the task is important. ↓

Mention the standard of the actions. ← Talk about actions which need to be completed. ← Explain the timeframe. ↓

Offer any assistance. → Mention you trust the other person. → Check for understanding. ↓

Confirm that they can and will do the task. ← Ask other person if they have any questions. ← Ask other person to summarise/paraphrase.

Figure 8: Delegation process

Let's see how Sofia handles this conversation with Sebastien.

SOFIA: Hi Seb, I've been reviewing our teams' strengths, and I think you would be a really good fit for a project I have in mind. The project involves taking the lead on our 'Fruity Banking' app and conducting a bit of a deep dive with the customer feedback. I believe you have the analytical skills for this.

SEBASTIEN: That sounds like an interesting challenge Sofia. Can you tell me a bit more please?

SOFIA: Well, the aim of this project is to deep dive into the surge of recent customer feedback that we have received regarding the app. We've noticed some recurring themes that we need to address to improve user satisfaction and engagement.

SEBASTIEN: Okay . . .

SOFIA: If we don't act on this feedback, we could potentially see a serious drop in our customer satisfaction scores and even start losing customers.

SEBASTIEN: Yes, this has serious implications for us.

SOFIA: We are planning to share the preliminary findings by the end of next quarter. That gives you enough time to analyse the feedback thoroughly and propose actionable improvements.

SEBASTIEN: Got it. So, what are the specific things you need me to do Sofia?

SOFIA: Well, I need you to categorise the feedback into common themes and then prioritise these on their impact and feasibility. Then, you would need to draft a proposal on the improvements we can make in the short and long term. Of course, each step would need to be backed up by solid data analysis to align with our app's strategic goals.

SEBASTIEN: That sounds interesting.

SOFIA: For this to be really effective, we will want to see how effectively the proposed improvements address the key issues that were mentioned in the feedback. We also need to see feasible solutions that could be realistically implemented by our tech team within our timeline and budget. Don't forget I am here to support you throughout the project. If you encounter any obstacles or need further clarification, don't hesitate to reach out.

SEBASTIEN: Thanks Sofia. I will definitely let you know if I have any other questions.

SOFIA: Great. Could you briefly summarise the main points of the discussion so that I can check that we are on the same page?

SEBASTIEN: Sure. I'm to lead the analysis of customer feedback on our app, categorise this feedback, prioritise improvements and suggest actionable steps by the end of next quarter. The purpose of all this is to improve user satisfaction and engagement.

SOFIA: Perfect summary Seb. Do you have any further questions or is anything still unclear?

SEBASTIEN: No, I think I'm good. I'm ready to get started Sofia.

SOFIA: Great. So just before we go, are you comfortable with taking on this project and do you feel like you have everything you need to make a start?

SEBASTIEN: Yes Sofia. I am confident that I can deliver the results you need.

SOFIA: Excellent! Let's make this project a success!

This approach ticked the SCARF boxes and motivated Sebastien to complete the project. Sofia's approach ensures that Sebastien is starting from the right place with all the expectations he needs as well as the firm belief that he can perform the task. Many managers are still unsure of how to delegate effectively and end up unwittingly (or wittingly) sabotaging their team's attempts to succeed. Some managers never get round to delegating at all!

Reluctance to Delegate

One significant reason that managers are reluctant to delegate is the fear of losing control. In a survey for the American Management Association, over 45% of managers expressed concern that tasks would not be done correctly if they were not done personally.[1] I'm guessing that Kelly was a respondent. At the heart of this is the manager clinging to the belief that they are better at tasks than their peers, which justifies their position in the hierarchy.

Secondly, another key factor is the perceived lack of time to train employees. According to Gallup, nearly one third of managers feel like they do not have the time to teach others or believe it is faster to do the task themselves than delegate.[2] But delegating isn't directing! Maybe managers feel they don't have the time for the delegation conversation? This is often driven by their need to focus on BAU, which in turn leads them to being constantly reactive and overstressed. This can lead to Kelly-esque frustration and inadvertent put downs of team members.

Thirdly, trust is a key factor that impacts managers' reluctance to delegate. Data from the Institute of Corporate Productivity (ic4P) states that nearly 46% of companies surveyed cite a 'lack of trust in employees' ability to execute tasks as a significant barrier to delegation.[3] This lack of trust might stem from not knowing their team members, negative past experiences or their own beliefs and need to control (Theory X).

Furthermore, a study by the Harvard Business Review points out that many managers struggle to grasp what delegation is. They fear that delegating tasks may make them look less capable or that they are simply Tai-Chi-ing (offloading) work. Approximately, 40% of the managers who were surveyed admitted to concerns about delegating as they might seem like they are shirking work responsibilities.[4] I can corroborate these findings from my own experiences when coaching managers. Often, managers will start a coaching conversation explaining that time is the main issue for them to achieve their more strategic goals. But when we dig deeper, the lack of time is often due to a reluctance to delegate. Dig deeper, and you find that reluctance to delegate stems from not wanting to appear like they are 'not busy' to their peers. They fear that their peers will think their boss is slacking, and this might trigger issues of relatedness and fairness, alienating the manager from the team.

Finally, I firmly believe that some managers are reluctant to delegate as they are unsure of what to do if they are not sucked into everyday BAU. Perhaps they fear the future, and so focus on the familiar ground below their feet. We will discuss what managers should be doing later in the book and how they should be spending more time 'thinking big'.

Theory Y and Delegation

Theory Y managers are best suited to delegate as they inherently believe in the potential and motivation of their team. They believe that employees are capable of self-direction and self-control and that their duty is to empower them. This lends itself to the manager desiring the success of their team to reinforce these beliefs and is coupled with a *growth mindset*, which does not fear the success of others.

Contrast this with the Theory X mindset, which believes that people need to be pushed and micromanaged as they are essentially lazy. This is likely to lead to a culture of managers giving poor instructions and self-sabotaging their team members to justify their beliefs. And this becomes a vicious circle. Every time Kelly's team member falls short, the clarion voice of her subconscious reiterates the message that she's better to do things herself. The problem with this approach is that it limits growth whilst maintaining Kelly's fixed belief that she is superior. Over time it may well end up that she's the smartest person in the room.

Chapter Echo

The intercom sound announces his PA, Trevor, asking him to sign off on some documents. Rupert ushers in the young man who always seems to be on his tiptoes. Leafing through the documents, Rupert sees board papers, budget approvals and a dozen or so more documents that need his signature.

As his pen hovers over yet another signature line, Rupert is struck by the amount of time he has spent signing these documents. He wonders if there might have been a better way and whether he has bottlenecked progress by not trusting others. But he is the CEO, though … right?

Key Takeaways: Chapter Five

1. Understanding Delegation

- Delegation is a strategy for managing highly skilled and motivated individuals by assigning them responsibilities that match their competencies, fostering further growth and autonomy.

- Effective delegation involves more than assigning tasks; it includes setting clear goals, providing necessary resources and maintaining regular check-ins.

2. Clear Goals

- Clear goals are foundational to successful delegation, providing a roadmap for what needs to be accomplished and the standards for success.

- Without clearly defined expectations, even skilled and motivated individuals may struggle to meet objectives.

3. Regular Check-ins

- Regular check-ins are essential, not to micromanage, but to offer support, feedback and necessary adjustments.

- These meetings help keep the project on track and allow managers to address any concerns or changes in scope, reinforcing that the team member is not alone in their efforts.

4. Balancing Autonomy and Support

- Effective delegation recognises the balance between granting autonomy and providing necessary support.

- Managers must ensure alignment with broader organisational goals while leveraging the skills and motivations of capable team members.

5. Common Mistakes in Delegation

- Vague instructions and lack of guidance can lead to misunderstandings and subpar performance.

- Delegating tasks without providing necessary tools or clear expectations often results in failure and frustration for both the manager and the employee.

6. Best Practices in Delegation

- Providing a comprehensive overview of the task, including clear goals, expectations and the critical role of the task in the organisation's strategy.

- Maintaining open lines of communication, encouraging questions and offering resources and examples to support the task completion.

7. SCARF Model in Delegation

- Linking the delegation process to the SCARF model (Status, Certainty, Autonomy, Relatedness, Fairness) enhances its effectiveness.

- Each step of the delegation process can address these elements, making the task more meaningful and motivating for employees.

8. Steps for Effective Delegation

- Mention why you are delegating to this person (Status).

- Talk about the purpose of the task (Certainty).

- Explain the importance and potential consequences of the task (Certainty and relatedness).

- Set a clear deadline (Certainty).

- Detail the required actions (Certainty and autonomy).

- Set quality standards (Certainty and fairness).

- Offer assistance and make it clear that you are available to help (Relatedness).

- Express trust and confidence in the team member's abilities (Status and autonomy).

- Check for understanding and ask the team member to summarise the task (Certainty).

- Invite questions and ensure mutual understanding (Relatedness and autonomy).

- Confirm that the team member can and will do the task (Autonomy and certainty).

9. Overcoming Reluctance to Delegate

- Common barriers include fear of loss of control, time constraints for training, lack of trust in employees' capabilities and concerns over perceptions of responsibility.

- Recognising the long-term benefits of delegation, such as enhanced team capacity, improved time management and a more skilled workforce, helps overcome these barriers.

10. Theory Y and Delegation

- Theory Y managers believe in the potential and motivation of their employees, making them well-suited to effective delegation.

- They see their role as facilitators who empower their team, fostering a supportive environment that enhances overall team performance and job satisfaction.

Reflection Questions

- What makes you reluctant to delegate more?

- How is not delegating impacting your work?

MOTIVATING

Every sheet of paper has two sides.

—Thai Proverb

REFLECTION TASK: MOTIVATING

Instructions: Rate each statement on a scale from Strongly Disagree (1) to Strongly Agree (5).

Statement	Strongly Disagree (1)	Disagree (2)	Neutral (3)	Agree (4)	Strongly Agree (5)
1. I praise team members based on their effort and growth, rather than innate talent.					
2. I give grandiose titles to top performers without focusing on their efforts.					
3. I regularly introduce more complex and stimulating tasks to maintain interest and enthusiasm.					
4. I assume that if I find a task challenging, it will be equally difficult for everyone.					
5. I provide specific, actionable feedback to help team members overcome obstacles and improve their skills.					

Statement	Strongly Disagree (1)	Disagree (2)	Neutral (3)	Agree (4)	Strongly Agree (5)
6. I give vague feedback without offering specific areas for improvement.					
7. I discuss the resources and support team members might need when assigning challenging tasks.					
8. I expect team members to figure out how to overcome obstacles on their own without guidance.					
9. I acknowledge team members' achievements before offering suggestions for improvement.					
10. I criticise mistakes without recognising achievements.					
11. I involve team members in setting goals and developing action plans for their improvement.					
12. I believe motivation should solely come from the individual's intrinsic drive.					

Read the chapter before you check your answers on p. 263

The Need to Motivate

Think about the last time you made a goal or a plan and set about the task with great enthusiasm. At some point in that journey to achieving your goal, you will have experienced being demotivated. Maybe you called into question the purpose of your goal or perhaps a new goal emerged that was more urgent or compelling. Or maybe a setback in your attempts to reach your goal derailed you.

If we remember our matrix, you may remember that the manager plays the role of motivator for employees who have the ability but have lost the drive to complete a task. This motivator's job is to reignite the spark in their team members to propel them back into action.

There are several ways that a manager can reignite this spark. First, praise shows recognition for the value team members bring to the organisation and the effort they have put in. But praise must be frequent and worded carefully as we will explore later.

Another approach to motivate team members is to increase challenge. This may be an effective strategy if a team member is becoming complacent or completing a mundane part of a project or task. This increase of challenge can become a motivator in itself and potentially lead the employee back to a more engaged state.

Finally, constructive feedback can be a way for managers to turn potential setbacks into opportunities for growth and change. Of course, constructive feedback must be given sensitively, and managers should remember SCARF as a principle to avoid further demotivation.

By combining praise (recognition), challenge and constructive feedback managers can foster an environment where their team are continuously challenged, supported and appreciated, ultimately leading to higher levels of job satisfaction and productivity.

KELLY

At Mango Bank, feedback from Kelly is a hard-won prize and team members can go for weeks without even a trace of acknowledgement. When she offers praise, Kelly is known for her distinctive style of recognition for her team. One feature of this is her habit of imposing titles on her top performers and using these in front of others. For example, you might hear Kelly call Ju-Hyun 'the creativity guy' or declare that Lilly the 'analytical wizard will save the day'.

Kelly assesses challenges through her own lens. She believes that if she finds a task challenging it must be equally difficult for everyone else. You might hear her say: 'I struggled with this so it will push you to your limits', as she briefs a team member. Her team often exchange quizzical glances, knowing that their skills and perspectives vary greatly. But they rarely challenge Kelly's assumptions.

And so, Kelly, much like a traditional parent, offers praise for excellence and relates the challenges of her 'children' to her own experience. Picture eyes rolling as she starts a conversation with: 'In my time ...'.

When it comes to giving constructive feedback, Kelly doesn't hold back. She relates her own experience and rolls out a list of suggestions and personal advice. Positioning herself as the expert on everything, Kelly antagonises even her most staunch followers, leaving them gasping for air like drowning swimmers reaching for the surface. Kelly also has an almost photographic memory and can pull examples of mistakes or poor performance from the depths of her memory and ready to be used as evidence.

SOFIA

In stark contrast, Sofia's approach to motivation is thoughtful, inclusive and frequent. She offers praise for effort and growth rather than for talent. She doesn't always wait for a project to be completed to say something positive to a team or team member. For instance, she might offer some praise to her talented Cambodian team member, Rithy. Rather than call out his talent or fixed abilities, you might hear Sofia say something like: 'Rithy, I'm really impressed by how much effort that you have put into developing our new marketing strategy. Your growth has been remarkable.' Sofia also considers the skill level of her team and increases the level of challenge for them accordingly. As she does this, Sofia will work on increasing their self-belief that they can achieve the task. When giving constructive feedback, Sofia will focus on the future and encourage input from her team members. This reluctance to position herself as the expert makes her more relatable and her team are comfortable to be open about how they can improve. This focus on growth keeps her team engaged at work. Sofia knows how to challenge even her most talented team members, pushing them back into the delegation quadrant of our matrix.

Feedback

Feedback, whether it is praise or constructive feedback, is essential for people to feel engaged at work. According to Gallup, frequency is a key factor for giving feedback. In fact, according to a Gallup poll, people who receive feedback weekly are 5.2 times more likely to strongly agree that they receive meaningful feedback. Furthermore, respondents stated that they are 3.2 times more likely to be motivated to do outstanding work. And finally, that old chestnut – 2.7 times more likely to be engaged at work.[1] So, frequency of feedback matters. And yet, in some companies I have worked with, feedback is kept locked inside a little wooden box until the six-month or yearly appraisal. Not very engaging.

Praise and Growth

Let's circle back to 1998, and an experiment that Carol Dweck and her team conducted on 400 fifth grade students in the United States.[2] During the experiment the children were given an IQ test to complete. Afterwards, the children were randomly divided up to receive two different types of praise. One group were praised based on their ability or talent and were told 'you must be smart at this'. The other group were praised for their effort, 'you must have worked really hard'. The children were then given a more challenging task and Dweck and her team noticed something remarkable. The children who had been praised for their effort were more likely to embrace the challenges of the new test and try harder. Furthermore, they were willing to persist even when they made mistakes. In contrast, the children who were praised for their intelligence tended to give up more easily and showed less enjoyment in the task. The experiment suggested that the way we praise our children (parent readers take note) can affect their outcomes. Children who are considered 'smart' or 'talented' are less likely to take risks and enjoy challenges. They become afraid to risk losing their title of being smart or talented and develop a fixed mindset.

But what implications does this have for managers?

Well, managers like Kelly tend to praise the abilities and intelligence of their team. They do this as a way of building relatedness and making their team feel valued. All good. Except that, if you are brilliant at something or an expert, you develop a bit of an ego. This makes you less willing to embrace challenges and become very resentful of failure. These are the people you hear blaming everyone else except themselves when things go wrong. They are attached to their *status* to the extent that they will play it safe to protect it. In the long run, this stifles their growth, and they achieve far less than they were capable of. Remember the story of William James Sidis? One wonders what he might have achieved if he had been able to adopt more of a growth mindset. When we give praise, we might be wise to avoid the Kelly style of praise:

'You are a natural at this'.

'You're such an amazing problem-solver'.

'Stephanie is our creative genius!'

'You can do this standing on your head, Ismail'.

Instead, if we follow Sofia's lead, we can word praise like:

'You've made great progress because of your consistent effort'.

'Your strategy and persistence were instrumental in solving that problem'.

'I'm impressed with the number of creative ideas you generated Stephanie'.

'It's clear that your hard work and tenacity have helped you really master this, Ismail'.

You might think that this is obvious but watch how you give feedback to your children (if you are a parent). It seems ingrained in us to want to praise our children with these badges, like: 'you are so smart Lisa' or 'you are brilliant Ganesh'. And yet, these badges may be the start of developing a fixed mindset in our kids.

One of the things that never ceases to amaze me is how people react to tests. Even adults in my training sessions are often incredulous when they score low in a test. They will come up with all sorts of excuses or even express their resignation. They are used to being experts and so any test that tells them otherwise is viewed with scepticism. That is understandable. But this fixed mindset is often ingrained in people from school, where tests are used to designate your status. You then join a company, where appraisals and rating systems are used to rank you again. The problem with ratings is that when you are top, there is only one place to go, and that is down.

Perhaps a growth mindset is really an acceptance of our changing nature. The impermanence of things. Our attachment to ourselves and our sense of status can bring us pain. But if we celebrate the process and the journey, the destination becomes less valued. If you could be magically transported to the top of K2 (the world's second highest and notoriously difficult-to-climb mountain), would you have learned anything?

Flow and Challenge

The concept of 'flow' was introduced by Hungarian-American psychologist Mihaly Csikszentmihalyi (pronounced cheek-sent-me-high).[3] The idea of flow was a state of complete engagement or total focus. This could occur when people found the perfect balance of skill and challenge — a bit like playing your favourite computer game. This would be where hours would pass quickly, and you might forget the time completely. Have you ever experienced that at work? Where time went by so quickly, you wondered where it had gone? You might have been in a state of 'flow'. If team members become demotivated or bored, managers can increase the level of challenge to keep them engaged. However, managers must be careful not to push the challenge too high or they might risk inducing anxiety in their team members. You can't always expect your team to be in a flow state but setting them stretch goals and increasing challenge responsibly can be one way of doing this. Managers need to observe their team at work to identify whether they are demotivated. This does not mean to say that you start micromanaging, though. Look at people's energy at work. You can soon tell if someone is in a flow state, just by the level of concentration on their face. Leave well alone . . . as this is where great work happens.

A Lesson from Spiders

Have you heard the story of Anansi? Anansi was a mischievous spider who thought he was smarter and cleverer than anyone else. One day, Anansi decided that he would travel around the world and collect all its wisdom. And he would keep it in a big clay pot. The more he travelled, the more wisdom he collected until his pot weighed a tonne. Once the pot was full, Anansi decided to climb a tree to hide the pot so that he didn't have to share the wisdom and all its treasures.

Up he tried to clamber to the top of the tree where he might hide the wondrous clay pot. But each time the pot would bang off his spidery legs and force him to scuttle back down.

After many more attempts, Kweku Tsin, Anansi's son, shouted out: 'why don't you carry the pot on your back, father? It will easier for you to climb the tree!' At first Anansi ignored his son's suggestion and staggered back up the tree. After, several more failed attempts, Anansi finally tried his son's suggestion and was able to climb the tree with ease.

Just as he reached the top of the tree Anansi, jubilant, realised that he had travelled the world for wisdom, but the answer to his problem had been close to home. And in that instance, the branch holding his pot snapped, and Anansi's pot fell to the earth and shattered. The wisdom contained in the pot was carried off by the wind and spread throughout the earth.

The Power of Constructive Feedback

Like Kweku Tsin, managers can use constructive feedback as a powerful tool to help team members overcome obstacles. However, skilled employees may, like Anansi, be reluctant to take on this feedback and so conversations must consider psychological safety to ensure that these conversations have the best intended outcomes. The SCARF model, developed by Dr David Rock and the Neuroleadership Institute can help us design conversations that reduce potential friction and threats to our team members. This can help them to internalise the feedback and avoid seeing it as one-upmanship from their manager.

SCARF and Feedback

The SCARF model can be employed for giving feedback in the following ways.

STATUS

This is where we might acknowledge the employees' efforts and achievements. This reinforces their sense of value and competence that can reduce defensiveness upon receiving the feedback. We should remember what we learned about the growth mindset here and refrain from praising ability or talent here.

Example:

'The effort and dedication you put into the recent project really brought your strong analytical skills to light. The way you solve complex problems really adds value to the team.'

CERTAINTY

Provide clear and specific feedback on what was done well and what needs improvement. This reduces ambiguity and helps the employee with the path forwards.

Example:

'Your report was comprehensive and well-researched. However, I did get some feedback that the report was very dense and wordy at times.'

AUTONOMY

To enhance a feeling of autonomy, a manager can encourage input from the team member themselves. Furthermore, they can encourage them to take ownership of their own improvement process that fosters a sense of control.

Example:

'What do you think you could do to make your reports more visual?'

and

'Which areas of your report writing do you think you should focus on next?'

RELATEDNESS

To ensure that there is a sense of relatedness, the manager should express genuine interest in the team member's development and well-being. The manager can also share their own challenges and difficulties to increase relatedness.

Example:

'I appreciate the hard work you put into the project. I'm here to support you in any way that I can.'

FAIRNESS

Managers must not forget fairness. But how can you show fairness when giving constructive feedback? Here the manager may need to actively explain impartiality and use any objective benchmarks as guidelines if possible.

Example:

'I'm sharing this feedback because it aligns with our team's goals of continuous improvement. It's important for everyone, including myself, to receive feedback.'

The SCARF model can help managers make giving constructive feedback a less painful process. By focusing on the five domains, we can prevent the team member from becoming overly defensive and taking an adversarial stance with the manager. Of course, this process might not always be necessary. Employees who have a growth mindset may relish getting critical feedback and a manager who gives it to them straight. The manager themselves must know their people well enough to tailor the way they give constructive feedback. Furthermore, managers must be genuine in their intentions surrounding constructive feedback. Feedback should never be used as a means to belittle others or perpetuate control. It must be given as a way to help others grow and achieve their potential.

FEEDFORWARDS

Feedforwards is a concept that was introduced by Dr Marshall Goldsmith,[4] one of the world's foremost experts on coaching. The idea with feedforwards is that managers shift from focusing on the past, which we cannot change, to improving our future. This can significantly impact the way that people perceive advice. If this is given in a supportive environment, it can help people see the opportunity to improve themselves and encourage a growth mindset. Feedforwards is the opposite of feedback and designed to reduce the potentially negative frame of looking to the past. Ultimately, there's nothing more frustrating than someone who constantly reverts to a past that you cannot change.

Feedforwards can also work with managers and peers giving constructive suggestions on what someone can do to improve their performance or achieve a goal. In Dr Goldmith's model, this can involve small to large groups giving each other suggestions surrounding an issue or problem. This positive reframing makes the recipient less defensive as they look forwards rather than back.

For managers, feedforward can be something just as simple as changing the wording of our feedback.

FEEDBACK

'I thought you did great in the town hall. You spoke a little fast though...'

FEEDFORWARDS

'I thought you did great in the town hall. As an opportunity for next time, you can slow your delivery at times'.

Which one do you prefer? Small tweaks to how we communicate and the words we use can have a significant impact on our results.

CONTAGIOUS ENERGY

Have you ever been sat somewhere, a coffee shop or an airport waiting lounge, and seen someone laughing. Without knowing why they were laughing did you experience a sense of joy or perhaps smile to yourself? You did? Well, what is happening is that the neurons in your brain are mirroring the other person's. When we see someone expressing an emotion, our neurons fire in a similar pattern to the person experiencing the emotion. Like a mirror we subconsciously adopt the behaviours of the other person.

As a manager, it is important that we carry the energy of our team. If we are brimming with energy and passion, it might just rub off on our team. Conversely, if we are constantly tired and sombre, the energy in our office might reflect that too.

Chapter Echo

As Rupert prepares for his lunch appointment at Odette with an old friend, he ponders over a question that a local journalist had once asked him in an interview. 'What drives you, Rupert?' the journalist had asked. That one had stumped him. Such an obvious question, but he had never really thought about it. As Rupert catches a glimpse of himself in the elevator reflection, he remembers a saying his Thai friend had once told him: 'every sheet of paper has two sides'. Money and recognition drove him in the beginning perhaps ... but now it was a sense of responsibility ... something about legacy. 'Ping' the elevator chimes ...

Key Takeaways – Chapter Six

1. Motivating Skilled but Low-Motivated Employees

- This approach focuses on reigniting drive and engagement through recognition and increased challenges.

- Providing praise and acknowledging expertise boosts morale and reinforces employees' value to the organisation.

- Introducing more complex tasks helps maintain interest and enthusiasm, leveraging skills more effectively and fostering a motivated workforce.

2. Constructive Feedback

- Constructive feedback is essential for identifying and overcoming obstacles, turning setbacks into growth opportunities.

- Feedback should be specific and actionable, guiding employees in refining their skills and demonstrating the manager's investment in their professional growth.

- Delivered supportively, it emphasises strengths and potential for improvement, creating a positive and productive work environment.

3. The Importance of Praise

- Praising effort and growth, rather than innate talent, fosters a growth mindset, encouraging continuous improvement and resilience.

- Poorly worded praise can lead to a fixed mindset, where individuals avoid risks to protect their identity.

- Effective praise recognises progress and persistence, encouraging employees to embrace challenges and step out of their comfort zones.

4. Flow and Challenge

- The concept of 'flow' involves deep immersion and engagement in a task, achieved when the challenge matches skill levels.

- Effective managers maintain team motivation by raising the level of challenge to re-engage demotivated employees.

- Setting appropriate challenges prevents boredom without causing anxiety, fostering a productive and motivated team environment.

5. Unlocking Obstacles

- Constructive feedback helps improve performance by providing a clear path for growth and development.

- Utilising the SCARF model enhances the effectiveness of feedback delivery.

- Feedback should acknowledge achievements, provide clear and specific improvement areas, encourage ownership, build rapport and ensure fairness.

Reflection Questions

- Do you enjoy receiving constructive feedback? Why/Why not?

- What techniques do you use to motivate yourself?

DIFFICULT CONVERSATIONS

When we avoid difficult conversations, we trade short-term

discomfort for long-term dysfunction.

—Peter Bromberg

REFLECTION TASK: DIFFICULT CONVERSATIONS

Instructions: Rate each statement on a scale from Strongly Disagree (1) to Strongly Agree (5).

Statement	Strongly Disagree (1)	Disagree (2)	Neutral (3)	Agree (4)	Strongly Agree (5)
1. I address performance issues promptly rather than waiting until they become critical.					
2. I avoid difficult conversations to prevent conflict and maintain relationships.					
3. I approach performance discussions with empathy and respect for the employee's situation.					
4. I express my frustrations and anger during performance discussions to make a point.					
5. I provide specific examples and evidence of the performance issues during the conversation.					
6. I give vague feedback without offering specific examples or evidence.					

Statement	Strongly Disagree (1)	Disagree (2)	Neutral (3)	Agree (4)	Strongly Agree (5)
7. I work with the employee to develop a plan for improvement and offer necessary support.					
8. I leave the employee to figure out how to improve their performance on their own.					
9. I acknowledge the employee's strengths and past achievements before discussing areas for improvement.					
10. I focus the conversation on finding constructive solutions rather than assigning blame.					
11. I dominate the conversation without giving the employee a chance to share their perspective.					
12. I ensure that the conversation is one-sided, focusing only on the negatives.					

Read the chapter before you check your answers on pp. 264–265

The Necessity of Difficult Conversations

Difficult conversations may be required for team members who have become demotivated and unskilled. Many managers shy away from these conversations as they fear conflict or are concerned about losing relatedness with the individual. However, delaying these conversations can lead to negative consequences: the employee assumes their behaviour is unnoticed or accepted and continues their disruptive behaviour, which slowly starts to impact the team.

Engaging in difficult conversations is a vital skill for several reasons. Firstly, these conversations provide an opportunity for managers to address performance issues. Managers can clarify expectations and work with team members to try to identify areas of improvement. This approach can prevent the situation from worsening and highlight the manager's intention to develop others.

Secondly, these conversations can also help maintain team morale and productivity. If underperformance is left unaddressed, it might lead to resentment from other team members who might feel like they are 'picking up the slack'. Addressing this issue quickly signals to the team that the manager holds all team members accountable and can help others perceive a sense of fairness.

Finally, if handled well, difficult conversations can strengthen manager–employee relationships. If managers demonstrate that they are willing to listen and engage in honest and supportive conversations, they can further build trust and show that they are invested in the growth of their team. If handled effectively, difficult conversations can reignite the spark to motivate others to start learning and performing again.

KELLY

Kelly's approach to difficult conversations is a bit like a pressure cooker. She waits until the steam is practically whistling out of her ears before she engages in a difficult conversation. She bottles up her anger like a stuffed suitcase that you might take on a long journey, straining at the zips and ready to burst open at the slightest chance. Imagine Kelly, hard eyed and slightly red faced, cornering an unsuspecting team member. Jaw tightly clenched before she delivers a deluge of threats and a catalogue of poor behaviour. Wait a little longer and you will see fingers being pointed and voices raised.

'Do you even know what a deadline is?' you might hear her demanding, eyes ablaze. 'I promise you this, the next deadline you miss, you will be out of the building before your feet can touch the ground!' Her team members nod furiously and promise to change their ways. When the emotion of the moment dissipates and they have quietly pondered on how often their feet do actually touch the ground, resentment slowly builds.

Kelly's approach instils fear in her team, and this often leads to either an initial flurry of activity or an ugly standoff. Those who scurry back to their desk to work are driven by fear. But it doesn't last long.

What Kelly doesn't realise is that her Theory X approach is not addressing the root cause of the problem. Instead, her commanding style is providing short-term fixes rather than long-term solutions. Kelly, jubilant from her sense of power, mistakenly thinks that she is communicating assertively.

Let's take the unfortunate story of Max, a former star employee who once dazzled everyone with his productivity and moments of creative genius. Kelly, however, had failed to see the storm clouds that were gathering over Max's personal life. Max had been going through a difficult divorce that had left him feeling isolated and unstable. This had affected his performance, and Max had fallen behind in learning some of the bank's new systems. Rather than trying to dig deeper, Kelly let her frustrations simmer until she finally exploded.

'Max what has happened to you? You have really let the side down, and I won't tolerate slackers in my team!' Kelly shouted, her patience finally snapping.

Before Max had the chance to explain his situation, Kelly had made up her mind. In a display of her managerial power, Kelly removed Max from the team, hoping that it would be a stark reminder for other members. Max, stunned and dejected, packed up his five years of experience and left. He took with him years of experience and potential that could have been saved if Kelly had been more empathetic and attempted to find the root cause of the situation.

The heavy-handed tactics helped solidify Kelly's reputation as a fearsome regulator. As a result, it helped to reinforce a culture of fear and insecurity where the other team members couldn't help but wonder who might be next. Instead of driving performance, Kelly's behaviour had driven a wedge between her and her team, leaving a trail of anxiety and uncertainty.

If only Kelly could see that a bit of empathy might have salvaged the situation and helped retain a previously motivated and skilled employee. But as Kelly briskly walks the halls of Mango Bank, head held high, she wrongly thinks that her behaviour is a form of assertiveness, and she quietly prides herself on her ability to tackle challenging people head on.

SOFIA

In Sofia's oasis, difficult conversations are also not shied away from. However, Sofia doesn't wait until she's got plumes of smoke coming out of her ears before engaging in these conversations. Her approach is to balance the needs of her team and the business whilst attempting to empathise with her team members.

When Sofia notices a pattern of poor performance and senses that her team member's performance is waning, she addresses an issue promptly but thoughtfully. She makes sure her judgement is objective and gathers evidence to decide whether the need for a difficult conversation is justified or not. She listens to different stakeholders who interact with that team member to ensure that she is not biased in her judgement and gathers metrics to support her case.

One story illustrates how Sofia approaches these conversations proficiently. When she noticed that Sandeep, a previous top performer, had been missing deadlines and seemed distracted, she decided to have a 'difficult conversation'.

Finding a private space, Sofia spent a few minutes composing herself before the conversation began. She did some deep breathing and practised making herself present before the conversation. Just as she became aware of the low hum of the air con and the distant rumble of thunder, a knock on the door signalled the arrival of Sandeep.

Sofia began the conversation by explaining the difference between the expected standards and Sandeep's current performance.

'Sandeep, I've noticed that your performance has not been up to your usual high standards for some time now', Sofia continued in a composed manner. 'Can we talk about what's been going on? I want to try to understand if there is something affecting your work and see how I might be able to help.'

Sandeep felt respected and valued and decided to open up and about the struggles he had been going through. 'Actually, Sofia, I have been going through a tough time. My mother has been very ill, and it's been hard to juggle everything. I feel like I am not on top of things, and I've fallen behind in learning the new project management software.'

Sofia listened empathetically and attempted to match the energy of Sandeep. 'I'm sorry to hear that, Sandeep. Family is incredibly important, and I can see how your home situation is affecting your work. Let's work together to find a solution that can help you manage your work and also the situation at home. Would you be open to that?'

Sofia and Sandeep went on to discuss possible changes to Sandeep's workload and ways for him to learn the new software with his colleagues' help. Sofia ensured that Sandeep knew he had her support and together they charted a road map to help Sandeep through his challenges.

The approach had several benefits, it demonstrated to Sandeep that Sofia genuinely cared about him as a person rather than just an employee. Furthermore, it helped Sandeep regain his composure and focus on improvements without fearing potentially unfair repercussions.

In another story, Sofia tackled a very demotivated Charles – an older member of the team who had once been its backbone and the go-to for information on anything from processes to compliance regulations. When Sofia spoke to Charles, he was very defensive about his performance and unwilling to change. But when Sofia dug a little deeper, she found the cause of where the resentment was coming from. Charles had attended a training on using a new tracking software. During the session, the trainer (Celine) had unwittingly made Charles lose face in front of his younger peers for not knowing how to drag and drop items on his desktop. Feeling ashamed and with his status in tatters, Charles had recoiled inwards, quietly resenting the team. Technology had become a barrier for him and before long his performance at work was dropping. Sofia worked on assuring Charles of the value he brought and promised to support him. She also made a mental note to talk to Celine about handling different learners in her training.

After implementing additional one-to-one training and support, Sofia monitored Charles performance closely. When he slowly began to improve, Sofia gave him praise that focused on his effort and the strategies he used to learn the new tech. However, if Charles was not prepared to change his behaviour, Sofia was ready to have a candid conversation about the next steps and moving the issue towards the human resources department.

The Fear of Difficult Conversations

Kelly and Sofia provide examples of the stark contrast between a Theory X and a Theory Y manager's approach to difficult conversations. Although the difference in approach is reflected in the beliefs of the two managers, it is also driven by one key response: fear and how the two managers deal with it. Most managers that I speak to fear difficult conversations. They provoke a stress response in the majority of people that can lead to them either avoiding the situation or having a Kelly-type outburst in the corridor. At best, many managers are unable to think rationally in a difficult conversation and come out of it without the results they wanted.

Assertiveness

A common misconception about assertiveness is that it just involves being 'firm'. Sometimes, people associate Kelly with assertive behaviour. They might point to her ability to bulldoze her way into getting results as a sign of assertiveness. It is important to remember that assertiveness is the ability to express one's thoughts, feelings and needs, honestly and respectfully. However, assertiveness also involves balancing this with respect for the other person's rights and feelings. Assertiveness is not the same as aggressive behaviour, which disregards the rights and feelings of others, or passivity, which involves allowing others to dominate a conversation with their rights and feelings whilst being reticent about sharing your own.

Our behaviour when we feel threatened is driven by a fear response. This fear translates into our body producing surplus energy and preparing us to run away or fight. People who choose to run away are conflict avoidant and will usually adopt a passive style. This is not ideal for managers, as conflict is an inevitable part of managing any team. Aggression is for those managers who respond to conflict by wanting to fight. This will often manifest as the Kelly style of management, culminating in tantrums and shouting matches on the office floor. It's the kid screaming on the airplane about not getting to play with their toy. There is also a third style: manipulative behaviour. This manifests as the manager who wants to both fight and run away. Typically, these managers are the ones who will use a middle person to do their bidding for them. They will use jokes and sarcasm rather than confront an issue directly. This is the manager who says: 'good afternoon, Kevin' in a sarcastic way when Kevin arrives at the office an hour late for work, rather than addressing the behaviour directly.

Assertiveness involves attempting to override the body's response to stress, which leads to the fight-or-flight paradigm. As we saw with Sofia, she takes time to compose herself before the meeting with Sandeep, attempting to centre herself and not let her emotions run away. This ability to manage fear is fundamental to managers who want to lead by lifting.

Assertive Communication

Assertive communication is characterised by clarity and openness. It avoids ambiguity and helps promote a sense of certainty in the listener. This prevents any misunderstanding from arising and helps ensure both parties are on the same page.

Respect and empathy are fundamental to assertiveness. While being open and direct, assertiveness also respects the other person's viewpoints and values their input.¹ This helps to create a dialogue rather than a managerial monologue.

The assertive voice is calm and measured even in challenging situations. This control over emotions is challenging and managers need to be able to remain rational even when they are being baited or provoked. Managers can work on their assertive voice by ensuring that it is both powerful and calm.

Managers should also work on the words they use in difficult conversations. For example, it is common to hear managers complain about someone's attitude in a difficult conversation. 'I don't like your attitude, Mei Leng!' The problem with this kind of language is that it gives no explanation for that actual behaviour we want to change. After all, attitude is a pretty subjective comment. This is why we must gather evidence before a difficult conversation to ensure that our approach is as non-biased as possible.

Assertiveness is about confidence. Assertive individuals are confident in their rights and opinions. This confidence in turn allows them to express their views without needing to threaten others.

Assertiveness and Culture

You might be thinking that assertiveness does not sit well with Asian culture. The idea of high-context cultures, developed by cultural theorists like Hofstede,[2] suggest that traditional Asian cultures find assertiveness uncomfortable and prefer to use inferences surrounding the context and unspoken communication to make a point. It would certainly be culturally inappropriate for a subordinate to be assertive to a manager, for example. However, I would push back on this for several reasons. First, if the manager takes a more Theory Y approach to management, they will be less hierarchical and reduce the level of *power distance* between the manager and their reports. Secondly, if the manager role models this behaviour, and shows care for their team member, they might encourage more candid conversations. Finally, and perhaps most importantly, Asian business cultures are changing. Assertiveness is becoming recognised as an essential competence for leaders. The need for transparency is helping Asian culture refine its own blend of assertiveness, which balances direct communication with respect for cultural norms.[3]

The Assertive Difficult Conversation

In difficult conversations, clarity is paramount. Assertive conversations assure that issues are addressed openly without any 'beating around the bush'. For example, when a manager wants to address performance issues, the manager can explain the team member's current performance and the difference between the expected standards. This ensures that the team member has a clear and objective understanding of the gap in performance.

When the manager is empathetic, they allow the team member to express their side of the story. This gives the employee the opportunity to potentially justify their reasons for the drop in performance. In the case of Charles, this helps Sofia give the support he needs to regain his confidence.

When team members become angry or difficult, the assertive difficult conversation ensures that words are chosen thoughtfully and that the manager themself is not triggered to return to aggressive or passive behaviour.

Finally, the assertive approach facilitates a more collaborative strategy to difficult conversations. It helps the manager to try to understand the drivers behind the behaviour – the interests behind the positions. Once these are identified the manager can collaborate with the team member to identify a way forward. This problem-solving approach is at the heart of collaborative conflict management and can help turn seemingly unsolvable performance issues into renewed opportunities to build trust and engagement amongst employees.

Using a Process Approach

The CEDAR model[4] is a powerful tool to help managers structure their difficult conversations (Figure 9). Let's look at the different stages of the conversation.

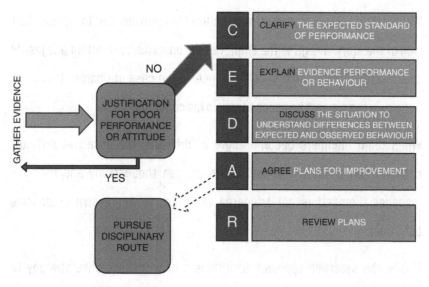

Figure 9: The CEDAR conversation framework

PRE-CONVERSATION PREPARATION

Before initiating the difficult conversation, it is crucial that managers gather evidence that supports the claims of poor performance. This evidence should be based on objective measures of feedback, such as performance metrics, attendance records or documented incidents. Gathering evidence ensures that the conversation is coming from an objective standpoint and helps mitigate preconceptions or biases.

Managers should also consider any external factors that might have impacted the team members performance. These may encompass some of Herzberg's hygiene factors that we discussed earlier: personal life issues, organisational change, working conditions, relationships with colleagues or job security. Understanding these factors can help the manager approach the conversation with a broader perspective and a heightened level of empathy.

CLARIFY THE EXPECTATIONS

In the opening of the conversation, the manager begins by clarifying the expectations of performance. This should be done in a sensitive and non-confrontational way. At this stage the manager needs to clarify what is expected in terms of performance, behaviour and outcomes. This step ensures that both parties have a clear understanding of the standards by which the performance is being measured. The manager should work on the *certainty* aspect of SCARF here by making it very clear what the standards are.

EXPLAIN THE OBSERVATIONS

Following the clarification of expectations, the manager then explains the observations or evidence that was collected during the preparation phase. The explanation should focus on specific facts and avoid any generalisations or personal judgements. Again, the manager should focus on *certainty*, ensuring that the information is relayed in a clear and unambiguous way.

DISCUSS THE DIFFERENCE

In this third phase of the conversation, the manager explains the gap in performance and attempts to find out any underlying reasons behind it. This stage provides an opportunity for the team member to share their perspective and any challenges they might be facing. If there have been external factors that have been impacting performance, the manager has the chance now to pivot their approach and take a more supportive role, focusing on how to tackle the issues collaboratively.

Agree on Plans for Improvement

If there aren't any external factors impacting performance, the manager shifts the conversation onto agreeing plans for improvement. This stage involves setting specific, achievable goals and concrete steps that the team member needs to take to improve. This does not necessarily have to be a formalised improvement plan, unless the conversation has been repeated before. The manager must ensure that the team member comprehends the plan and commits to it. The manager can help influence the domain of *autonomy* here by stating the agreement as a collaborative request rather than a fixed command.

If the team member does not agree to the plans for improvement, the manager calmly explains that they will need to raise the issue with human resources and ends the conversation. This sows the seeds of a disciplinary procedure and clearly shows the team member that there are consequences for their inaction.

Review

Finally, the manager and team member agree on a timeline to review progress. The manager should create achievable targets here, and clearly show the team member they are trying to be *fair*. The manager should reiterate that they have trust in the team member to turn the situation around and thus, influence their sense of *status*. Finally, the manager can offer any help or support and influence their sense of *relatedness*.

Sofia and Ganesh

Let's see how Sofia uses the CEDAR model to have a firm but fair conversation with a team member – Ganesh.

Pre-Conversation Preparation

Sofia has noticed a decline in Ganesh's performance over the past few months. She has gathered evidence of his performance including missed deadlines, decreased quality of work and even some feedback from his colleagues who have stated that Ganesh is uncollaborative. Sofia also considers any hygiene factors that might have influenced his performance but is unable to think of anything.

Clarify

SOFIA: Hi Ganesh. Thanks for taking the time to meet with me today. I wanted to discuss your performance over the past couple of months. Firstly, I wanted to remind you of your expected performance. The expectation is that you meet project deadlines and ensure a high quality of work.

Furthermore, the expectation is that you communicate effectively and collaborate with your team.

EXPLAIN

SOFIA: Obviously I have noticed several examples where this has not been the case. For example, the project reports for the past two months have missed the deadlines by several days. Furthermore, the quality of the work has not been up to your usual standard, and you have missed key sections in some of your reports. On top of that, I have received some feedback from your team members that there have been some difficulties with communication and collaboration.

DISCUSS

SOFIA: Ganesh, I really value you as a team member and you are capable of excellent work. Can you help me to understand what might be happening? I know there can be lots of things that can affect our performance. Is there anything specific that has been affecting your work performance recently?

GANESH: Well, actually yes Sofia. I've been struggling with some post-Covid symptoms. I've been feeling washed out and really tired at times. It's affecting my ability to find my focus on stuff.

SOFIA: I'm sorry to hear that, Ganesh. That sounds challenging and I can understand how it would impact your work. Your well-being is important, and I would like to ensure that we can provide you with support during this time. How can we adjust your workload and provide you support so that you can manage both your tasks at work and your health?

GANESH: Thank you, Sofia. I appreciate that. Perhaps I could have some flexibility with deadlines or some help with my current projects. That could really make a difference.

SOFIA: Absolutely, we can work on setting some more manageable deadlines or getting you some additional support.

AGREE PLANS

SOFIA: Moving forwards, let's agree on a plan to pair you with a colleague to provide support on your projects. And let's adjust some of the deadlines that won't impact our clients negatively. We'll review this arrangement regularly to ensure that it's working. Does this sound like something that could work for you?

GANESH: Yes, that sounds very helpful.

REVIEW

SOFIA: Great! We'll set up weekly check-ins to review your progress and make necessary adjustments. We'll try to make sure you are supported and can do your tasks without any added stress. If at any point you feel overwhelmed, don't hesitate to reach out.

Incorporating SCARF

In the above dialogue, Sofia attempts to make Ganesh feel psychologically safe by using the SCARF methodology in the conversation.

STATUS

Sofia acknowledges Ganesh's previous contributions and the value she thinks he brings.

CERTAINTY

Sofia provides clear information on her expectations and the next steps to move forwards.

AUTONOMY

Sofia involves Ganesh in developing the improvement plan and frames it as a request rather than a command.

RELATEDNESS

Sofia shows concern and empathy for Ganesh's predicament, helping to build trust and connection.

FAIRNESS

Sofia based her feedback on specific evidence and was transparent about the process which helped ensure the conversation felt fair.

The Leadership Route: An Optimistic View

The ideas in the book are built upon an optimistic view of human beings and their relationship with work. Perhaps the need for believing in the potential of people to do good is greater than ever. A key tenet to the leadership route is empathy and perspective taking. This can help us understand that drops in performance are natural and part of the cycle of work. We can't *always* be engaged or in a flow state. Sometimes, we are thrown a curve ball in life: an illness, the loss of a loved one, issues with our mental health or relationship issues. This can derail our progress and shift our focus causing us to lose the motivation or confidence and in turn our skills to perform what were once routine tasks.

If someone was once a good performer, it stands to reason that there should be a specific cause behind their decline in performance. These often come down to the following: organisational change, poor management practices or a lack of hygiene factors. Let's explore each of these factors.

ORGANISATIONAL CHANGE

Organisational changes like restructuring, changes in leadership or company strategy can significantly impact employee performance. These changes can disrupt any sense of *certainty* or routine and can lead to a danger or stress response, which in turn can lead to drops in team productivity. Managers must attempt to provide support and reassurance during turbulent times. This can include regular updates even when there is no new news to share. In some circumstances, employees have new reporting lines after changes take place. New managers often forget the importance of relatedness and skip the all-important bonding sessions to kickstart new team formation.

POOR MANAGEMENT

Poor management can lead to a decline in performance. Overly controlling or Theory X managers can cause team members to feel inhibited and the lack of autonomy can create boredom or even resistance. Furthermore, if an employee is not receiving adequate feedback or support. This can lead to disengagement as employees lack recognition or the sense of achievement they need to feel involved. Over time, this can lead to apathy and the drive to perform, learn and unlearn may dissipate. Managers who choose the leadership route are constantly striving to improve their own practices. They are always looking for ways to help team members thrive. When team members actively resent the management, they are much more likely to stop performing and resisting. They will be resistant to changes and learning because they inherently mistrust management. Why would you learn from someone who you feel doesn't have your best interests at heart?

LACK OF HYGIENE FACTORS

Hygiene factors, a term popularised by Herzberg, are elements of the workplace that do not cause engagement but may lead to general satisfaction. If they are lacking, they may in turn lead to general workplace dissatisfaction. Hygiene factors like work–life balance or conditions at work if not adequate might lead to frustration or demotivation. Managers who follow the leadership route take a general interest in their employees and try to ensure that these conditions are met. Where managers are unable to provide hygiene factors, they may need to go out of their way to provide support and show empathy to team members. If team members feel dissatisfied with salaries, managers may need to lobby key stakeholders for an increase in pay. If this is not possible, they may need to streamline their team to allow more slack in their budgets to offer more pay.

Looking for a Root Cause

When a previously good performer shows signs of decline, the manager should attempt to investigate what has caused the drop in performance. This provides a much more constructive approach than jumping to conclusions about capabilities or commitment. If managers ask the right questions and show genuine concern, they may be able to uncover the root cause behind the poor performance. However, this is unlikely to work if the manager is perceived as controlling. Team members would be unwilling to share their problems with a Theory X manager who they feel may use anything they say in evidence against them.

Temporary Drops and Bad Hires

It is important to distinguish between temporary drops in performance and employees whose performance is poor from the outset. If an employee has always been poor, it is probably a sign of a bad hire or mismatch between the employee's skillset and the necessary requirements for the role. In such cases, managers might need to consider whether extra training, reassignment or even termination might be the best approach.

The Role of Empathy and Support

The leadership route emphasises the role of empathy and support in dealing with performance issues. Instead of defaulting to a punitive approach, managers seek to understand and support employees. This includes listening actively, offering constructive feedback and collaborating on solutions that address the root cause of performance issues.

If managers offer a supportive environment, they may be able to help employees overcome obstacles and return to previous levels of performance. This sets a powerful precedent for other team members who perceive the manager as fair and genuinely invested in the welfare of the team.

Hard and Soft

Leading by lifting isn't all about being a walkover. Some of you might be thinking this approach would inevitably lead to people taking advantage of the manager and manipulating them.

The Chinese idiom 刚柔并济 [gāng róu bìng jì] or combing hardness and softness is a good descriptor for the manager who chooses the leadership route.

These are leaders who can make difficult decisions and have tough conversations. Their empathy and optimism cannot be confused with weakness. On the other hand, their negative experiences with certain employees don't lead them towards generalisations or push them towards the negative mindset of Theory X. They remain optimistic about their team and the principles of Maslow and Herzberg.

The need to manage conflict is more pertinent than ever as the evolution of management from being control-based to enablement accelerates. As managers can no longer rely on traditional position power by default, they must enhance their conflict management skills and assertiveness. This means working on collaborative problem-solving skills and looking for win–win outcomes where possible.

Chapter Echo

Rupert was delighted to get back to the office. The food in Odette's had been fabulous and his old friend Bernard had furnished him with some interesting stories of their small clique of friends. To Rupert's discomfort he had brought up Graham, an old foe but friend of the rest of the group. Rupert and Graham had once been good friends, setting up a small consultancy in the early 1990s. They had fallen out over their inability to tackle the sensitive issue of dealing with an important customer who had been causing trouble for months.

Rupert had always been cautious and diplomatic, preferring to sidestep conflict and avoid any direct confrontation that might put the newly founded consultancy at risk. In contrast, Graham preferred to tackle things with more open and transparent communication. Their differences had escalated into a heated argument, culminating in Graham walking away and leaving Rupert at the tiller of the fast-sinking firm. The rift between Graham and Rupert had grown over the years with each man thinking they were in the right.

Hearing Bernard talk about Graham with such positivity had triggered Rupert. He wondered what could have been if they had managed to find the solution to their differences. Perhaps it was time to reach out to Graham. A call … maybe a WhatsApp . . . an email perhaps. He glanced at his watch. It was already 2.00 pm. Time to crack on . . .

Key Takeaways – Chapter Seven

1. Importance of Addressing Difficult Conversations

- Engaging in difficult conversations promptly is essential for addressing performance issues directly and constructively.

- Delaying these discussions can lead to more significant problems, as employees might assume their behaviour is unnoticed and continue or escalate disruptive actions.

- These conversations help maintain team morale and productivity by ensuring that all team members are held to the same standards.

2. Benefits of Difficult Conversations

- They provide an opportunity to clarify expectations and work with employees to identify areas for improvement.

- Promptly addressing underperformance prevents the situation from worsening and shows the manager's commitment to the employee's development.

- These conversations can strengthen the manager–employee relationship when handled with empathy and respect.

3. Assertiveness in Difficult Conversations

- Assertiveness involves expressing thoughts, feelings and needs directly, honestly and respectfully.

- It strikes a balance between aggression and passivity, enabling clear and open communication that respects both parties.

- Assertive communication is characterised by clarity, respect, empathy, calmness and confidence.

4. Using the CEDAR Conversation Approach

- **Clarify the expectations:** Clearly outline what is expected in terms of performance, behaviour and outcomes.

- **Explain the observations:** Present specific and factual evidence of performance issues without personal judgments.

- **Discuss the difference:** Explore the gap between expected and current performance, understanding any underlying reasons.

- **Agree on plans for improvement:** Set specific, achievable goals and outline steps for improvement, involving the employee in the process.

- **Review:** Regularly check progress and provide feedback to ensure the employee stays on track.

5. Incorporating the SCARF Model into CEDAR Conversations

- **Status:** Acknowledge the employee's contributions and skills.

- **Certainty:** Provide clear and consistent information about expectations and feedback.

- **Autonomy:** Involve the employee in developing the improvement plan.

- **Relatedness:** Build rapport and show empathy.

- **Fairness:** Ensure the conversation and actions are perceived as fair.

6. Leading by Lifting

- Recognises that performance drops often have underlying causes, such as organisational changes, poor management practices or a lack of hygiene factors.

- By investigating these causes and providing empathetic support, managers can help employees overcome challenges and improve their performance.

- This approach builds a stronger, more resilient team and contributes to a positive and productive workplace.

Reflection Questions

- How did you feel the last time you had a difficult conversation?

- Did you do or say anything you now regret?

COACHING

Coaching is unlocking a person's potential to maximize

their own performance.

—John Whitmore

REFLECTION TASK: COACHING

Rate each statement on a scale from Strongly Disagree (1) to Strongly Agree (5).

Statement	Strongly Disagree (1)	Disagree (2)	Neutral (3)	Agree (4)	Strongly Agree (5)
1. I listen actively and encourage the employee to share their thoughts and feelings.					
2. I often share my experiences and solutions to guide the employee.					
3. I ask open-ended questions to help the employee explore their own solutions.					
4. I tend to give direct advice on what the employee should do.					
5. I create a safe space for the employee to reflect on their own actions and ideas.					
6. I focus more on telling rather than asking during coaching sessions.					
7. I help the employee identify their own strengths and how to leverage them.					

Statement	Strongly Disagree (1)	Disagree (2)	Neutral (3)	Agree (4)	Strongly Agree (5)
8. I often take control of the conversation to ensure it stays on track.					
9. I encourage the employee to set their own goals and action plans.					
10. I rely on my own expertise to solve the employee's issues.					

Read the chapter before you check your answers on pp. 265–266

Coaching: The Fifth Element

Coaching stands as a fifth approach to empowerment which takes place in one-to-one conversations between the employee and manager. Coaching conversations are designed to help individuals realise their potential and to grow. Typically coaching involves a series of conversations that focus on overcoming obstacles or problems to help employees maximise their potential. However, there are several ways that managers and employees might define coaching. We will investigate the main split between two key ideas of coaching in this chapter.

Let's return to our two managers at Mango Bank to explore their different approaches to coaching.

KELLY

Kelly uses a directive style of coaching in her conversations with her young protégé, Liam. The approach involves Kelly, perched on the end of her chair, eyes blazing with intensity, giving Liam specific advice and teaching him what to do in certain situations. This approach helps Kelly maintain her status as an expert and aligns with Liam's beliefs about what coaching involves. A win–win?

Kelly starts off every conversation by clearly outlining the problems that Liam is having. She then proceeds to offer concrete action steps and advice on how to solve these problems. You can think of Kelly as giving Liam a recipe book for success, except the secret ingredient is always *more Kelly*.

Kelly's approach to coaching is rooted in the belief that, as she is the manager, she should have the solutions for the problems her team are facing. In coaching conversations, Kelly often finds herself in teaching mode, pouring out years of knowledge and experience that she has accumulated. At first, Liam feels honoured to be the receptacle for Kelly's downloads, soaking up the insights and basking in being Kelly's apprentice. At the end of the day, who wouldn't want to be spoon fed solutions like a toddler at lunch time?

But as time passes, Kelly's directive approach to coaching conversations builds a dependency for Liam to hear the answers. He starts to rely heavily on Kelly for guidance and to solve problems, often feeling lost or overwhelmed when he has to make a decision for himself.

Furthermore, Liam doesn't take ownership for the solutions Kelly provides. When these solutions occasionally fail, Liam tends to shift the blame onto Kelly, rather than reflecting on what he could do to improve the approach or get better results. In the end, it's a bit like relying on a GPS that sometimes takes you to the wrong destination. We know it might not work but have become reliant on using it.

As a result of this dependency, Liam's growth and development slowly becomes stunted. As he consistently receives ready-made solutions from Kelly, Liam does not explore his own problem-solving or decision-making abilities. He rarely has time to self-reflect as the pace of the coaching doesn't allow him any time for reflection. As a result, Liam is running on a treadmill, he's moving but not getting anywhere and is unable to transform himself as his conversations with Kelly haven't increased his self-awareness.

SOFIA

Sofia's approach looks entirely different. Let's take the example of the conversations that she has with one of her direct reports – Madupe. Her approach involves exploring Madupe's problems together, rather than providing direct advice. This method is initially more challenging for both coach and coachee, but ultimately develops a sense of ownership and empowerment in Madupe's learning journey.

Sofia begins each conversation by allowing Madupe the space to discuss something that matters to her at work. She listens deeply to Madupe's challenges, mirroring her intensity and emotion, while asking questions that help Madupe reflect on the issues. There are moments of silence in conversations as both Madupe and Sofia reflect on the situation and way forward.

Sofia's approach is rooted in the belief that people grow best when they discover their own solutions. At first, Madupe finds this process frustrating as she feels like Sofia is withholding advice. But as she learns to work with the process, she develops a sense of autonomy and ownership in her journey.

When the solutions that she finds with Sofia work, Madupe feels a sense of accomplishment and growth. Alternatively, when these solutions fail, Madupe reflects on how she might adjust or improve her strategy without rushing to blame Sofia.

There are, of course, times when Sofia's approach doesn't lead to any specific breakthrough. This proves to be frustrating for Madupe as she is forced to come up with the answers herself. Nevertheless, these moments of struggle are when Madupe learns the most, building resilience and problem-solving skills that are crucial for her development. In addition, by consistently finding her own solutions, Madupe develops her confidence and learns to become more innovative. This fuels her potential for growth as she discovers both her strengths and strategies.

Sofia's approach, whilst challenging at the start, yields powerful long-term results. Madupe becomes more self-reliant and innovative, capable of solving the obstacles that stand between her and high performance. Sofia has lifted Madupe, rather than pull her up. It builds a powerful bond between the manager and her team member, which further increases loyalty and trust.

Evaluating the Two Approaches

DIRECTIVE COACHING (KELLY'S APPROACH)

The benefits of directive coaching are that it includes providing clear solutions and actionable steps. This can be time efficient and often fulfil a team member's expectation of what coaching is. It helps the manager to maintain their status as expert and can be a powerful way of increasing their confidence as a leader. If you invested a lot of time and effort in showing people how much of an expert you are, their expectation would be that you will teach them. If you don't, they might feel that you are withholding solutions from them as a way of maintaining your own power.

On the flip side, the approach can create a dependency in team members who get used to simply being told what to do. Furthermore, team members are less inclined to take ownership of their work, preferring to be spoon fed. This helps them to blame the manager when solutions fail as they don't feel responsible for outcomes. There is also the possibility of misalignment where the solutions of the manager are not relevant to the specific needs or context of the team members, leading to further frustration. Finally, the directive approach to coaching limits personal growth and transformation as team members are unable to find their own solutions to their problems.

Finally, directive coaching looks pretty similar to directing in our matrix. The difference might be that traditional directing involves focusing on a task, whereas directive coaching focuses on problem-solving. However, both approaches involve knowledge transfer from manager to employee based on the expertise of the manager.

NON-DIRECTIVE COACHING (SOFIA'S APPROACH)

Non-directive coaching allows employees to take full responsibility for their solutions and decisions, which helps to foster a deep sense of engagement and accomplishment. The approach also helps team members develop confidence and critical thinking as the coach assists them in challenging assumptions and limiting self-beliefs. The autonomy of the conversations helps to fuel their potential for transformation and growth, allowing them to discover their strengths and strategies.

The risks of non-directive coaching are that it can be challenging and time-consuming for both the manager and team member. The team member might never arrive at a solution to their problem, which can lead to frustration and questioning the benefits of the conversations. However, even without finding a solution, the coachee is forced to reflect on their own thinking process and challenge the assumptions and beliefs that they have. This is a fundamental step in transformation and change.

It is important to note that for most professional coaching bodies, such as the International Coaching Federation (ICF), coaching is always non-directive. The ICF defines coaching as 'partnering with clients in a thought-provoking and creative process that inspires them to maximize their personal and professional potential'.[1] This definition underscores the emphasis on the client's own resourcefulness and capabilities.

Example Conversations

Let's look at how a manager might use a directive and non-directive style in conversation with Budi – their coachee.

DIRECTIVE CONVERSATION

MANAGER: Let's talk about your project work Budi. How's that going?

BUDI: Well, I'm still far off from completing it …

MANAGER: It sounds like you're struggling to manage your time effectively. You need to identify the specific tasks that are taking up too much time and consider which of these you can delegate to your team.

BUDI: Well, I just don't have enough time . . .

MANAGER: You have to make time, Budi. Start by prioritising your tasks. Focus on the high-impact ones and delegate the routine, day-to-day activities to your team members.

BUDI: The current workload is crazy! I'm really busy with the BAU stuff and don't have time to focus on any project work. I guess I need to delegate more . . .

MANAGER: Exactly. Delegate the BAU tasks. As a leader, it's important to empower your team and not take everything on yourself. This will help free up your time for critical project work.

BUDI: But I think as a leader, I need to be hands-on in very busy times. Show the team that I'm supporting them. I don't want them to think I'm slacking when the business is super busy.

MANAGER: Your team won't think you're slacking if you clearly communicate why you're delegating. Make it clear that their involvement is critical for their development and the business's success. You need to trust your team more and delegate.

BUDI: Yes, I see your point.

MANAGER: Good. Start delegating more of the BAU work today. Focus on what only you can do, which is driving this project to completion.

Non-Directive Conversation

MANAGER: What do you want to talk about today, Budi?

BUDI: I would like to talk about my project work. I'm still far off completing it . . .

MANAGER: What is the reason that you are far from completing it?

BUDI: Well, I just don't have enough time . . . (pause)

MANAGER: What is the reason that you don't have enough time? (pause)

BUDI: Well . . . the current workload is crazy! I'm really busy with the BAU stuff and don't have time to focus on any project work. I guess I need to delegate more . . .

MANAGER: So, what's stopping you from delegating more? (silence)

BUDI: Well . . . I think as a leader I need to be hands-on in very busy times. Show the team that I'm supporting them. I don't want them to think I'm slacking when the business is super busy.

MANAGER: What makes you say that you would be slacking?

BUDI: Well . . . no I would be doing my project work . . . which is really important too.

MANAGER: Yes . . . how do you know your team would think that you were slacking? (pause)

BUDI: Well . . . I don't.

Which of these approaches do you think you would prefer? You might prefer the directive approach, right? But what would happen if you delegated those tasks? Would that help you deal with the persistent doubt that you are letting your team down?

Non-Directive Coaching and Theory X

Non-directive coaching can be a challenge for Theory X managers because of the conflict between the beliefs a Theory X manager holds and the nature of non-directive coaching. Theory X managers believe that employees dislike work, avoid responsibility and require close supervision. As a result, these managers adopt a controlling style to ensure efficiency and productivity. In turn, this leads to a work environment where team members feel scrutinised and pressured, rather than supported or empowered.

Non-directive coaching is unlikely to work with Theory X managers as team members are expected to engage in open and honest discussions. It would be hard to open up to someone if you fear reprisal or judgement. Imagine telling Kelly that you are struggling with your workload because you are unable to assertively say 'no' to work requests. You would probably fear that your admission of weakness would be met with further criticism, punishment or even micromanagement rather than constructive support. If team members mistrust their manager's intentions, they may end up playing a kind of cat-and-mouse game in the coaching conversation. They might offer superficial compliance without revealing their real feelings or challenges. Furthermore, they will be unlikely to make themselves vulnerable, which can lead to a lack of genuine engagement and personal transformation.

When I have conducted training sessions, I've usually found that groups who have a good rapport and connection are much more likely to open up about their real problems than groups who are more reserved or uncomfortable with their peers. This is often indicative of the organisational culture as people are unused to presenting their authentic selves or overly attached to their expertise.

For team members who fear their manager, non-directive coaching may not be a suitable approach. The adoption of a non-directive approach by a Theory X manager would certainly arouse the suspicions of most team members. In the end, a wolf may lose its fur, but not its nature.

Non-Directive Coaching and Lifting

Theory Y managers trust their team's motivations and abilities and see them as partners in achieving organisational goals. They focus on empowerment and collaboration, which helps develop a trusting and supportive environment. There is a mutual respect between managers and team members that creates a conducive environment for non-directive coaching.

Theory Y managers believe that employees are intrinsically motivated by growth, achievement and recognition rather than just monetary reward or fear of punishment. Non-directive coaching helps team members tap into these intrinsic motivations by helping team members set their own goals and find their own ways to achieve success.

As Theory Y leaders model themselves as learners who have made and make mistakes, this encourages a culture of learning through experimentation, risk-taking and innovation. These are all qualities that can help team members feel comfortable enough to experience vulnerability in a coaching discussion. If the team members trust that the manager's intentions are positive, they will be far more likely to open up in conversation.

If team members feel that they can be open with their manager without fear of reprisal they may find that non-directive coaching is a powerful catalyst for personal transformation. Furthermore, the cathartic nature of having someone listen to them with complete focus can further build powerful bonds of trust between the manager and their subordinate.

Starting a Coaching Relationship

Even if a manager is Theory Y, a lifter, it is still crucial to clearly explain the concept of non-directive coaching to set the expectations of the coachee. This can help avoid any misunderstandings of what coaching is and how it differs from directing.

Managers should outline the principles of what non-directive coaching is and explain that the coachee will be responsible for finding their own solutions. They should connect this approach to the belief that it can encourage growth, autonomy, empowerment and personal transformation. They should also state that it can enhance problem-solving skills and enhance confidence. A pretty good sell for a conversation, right?

Following this, managers should spend some time clarifying the roles in the coaching relationship. The manager should explain that the coach's role is to listen actively and ask questions that provoke reflection in their coachee. The journey is one of mutual exploration, and the coach has no hidden motive to lead their team member in a particular direction. Conversely, the coachee's role is to reflect and explore solutions open-mindedly. They are responsible for their own growth during conversations, and they should avoid asking the manager for advice as this might not be suitable for their context.

Managers would also do well to explain to their team member that coaching is not always easy. It might be frustrating at first and that this frustration may give way to powerful insights about themselves and their path forward.

Finally, the manager should discuss how success will be measured in the coaching relationship. The manager can outline the goals and milestones collaboratively with the coachee in order to track the progress and ensure that conversations remain focused.

It is very important to align these expectations early in the relationship. For people who have not learned in this way, it can be an overwhelming experience at first. But if we set the expectations correctly, it can lead to a powerful journey for both the manager and the team member. Many organisations still misunderstand what coaching is and send their senior leaders into coaching sessions without educating them about what to expect. This can often end up with more cynical leaders feeling that the coaching is a waste of time.

EXAMPLE CONVERSATION

Let's look at a sample conversation between Sofia and Hafiz, as she models how the coaching relationship will work.

SOFIA: Hi Hafiz! Thanks for sitting down with me today. I wanted to discuss our coaching journey and make sure that we are on the same page. Have you had coaching before?

HAFIZ: Well . . . In my previous role I had a manager who gave me advice and kind of shared their experiences with me.

SOFIA: Ok. My approach to coaching is a little different Hafiz. Instead of me giving you advice or solutions, I will be working with you to help you find solutions yourself. With this approach, we can help you improve your own problem-solving skills whilst building your confidence and taking ownership of your growth. Does that make sense?

HAFIZ: Errr . . . Kind of . . . How exactly does it work?

SOFIA: Great question. Well, my role will be to listen to your ideas, ask questions and offer you support as you explore different solutions. For example, if you are having difficulties with a particular project, I won't give you my solution, rather I might ask 'What could you do differently?' or 'what have you not tried yet?'.

HAFIZ: I see . . . so you are not going to give me any answers directly?

SOFIA: Well, it's not about me not giving you answers. Rather, I want you to find solutions yourself. Furthermore, my solutions might not be relevant to you or your situation. I want to build your ability to handle future challenges independently. I will also be learning from you and how you think. It might help shed some light on my own challenges.

HAFIZ: Right . . . that sounds like it might be . . . challenging.

SOFIA: Yes, it can be challenging at the start Hafiz. But we don't grow without challenge, right? And I will be here to support you on every step of your journey.

HAFIZ: Ok . . . that makes sense. How are we going to measure progress?

SOFIA: Well, we will set specific goals together and we will discuss your progress in some of the sessions. We will see how you are developing, and we can adjust our approach if necessary.

Hafiz: That sounds good Sofia. I am willing to give it a try.

Sofia: Great! I'm excited to see where this journey takes both of us. Don't forget that I am here to support you, and you can reach out if you need any support. I believe in your potential Hafiz and together we can unlock it!

The Importance of Trust

For a non-directive coaching session to work, the team member must trust the manager. There are a few key ways that a manager can help instil trust in their team.

First, the manager must ensure that conversations with their team remain completely confidential. They must ensure that anything discussed within a coaching session will not be shared with other team members or more senior leaders unless explicitly agreed upon. The manager, by ensuring confidentiality, can help create a safe space where the coachee feels safe to be vulnerable and share their thoughts and emotions. Managers must stay committed to this idea of confidentiality to ensure that they build a strong foundation of trust.

Secondly, managers must prioritise coaching sessions. This means that they should avoid consistently cancelling or postponing sessions as this sends out a strong signal to the coachee that the sessions are not important. By sticking to scheduled sessions, managers show that they are prioritising the development of their team and that they are dedicated to the coaching process.

Furthermore, managers must stay present in the coaching sessions. This means avoiding checking their phones or showing that they are distracted. They should maintain eye contact where appropriate and show that they are thoughtfully responding to the coachee's concerns and ideas. This complete focus can be energetically tiring, as it requires the coach to be consistently present and avoid slipping into other thoughts. As the great Krishnamurti describes in The Book of Life 'there must be in listening an alert passivity'.[2] This level of focus from the manager can also help to retain a feeling of trust.

Finally, managers should follow through on any commitments that are discussed during coaching sessions. If a manager states that they will provide further feedback, resources or additional support, they must ensure that they deliver on these promises.

By ensuring confidentiality, prioritising sessions, remaining present and following through on commitments, managers can ensure that can build and maintain trust with their team members.

Rapport without Friendship

Many people believe that a good coach is really a good friend. I strongly disagree. To coach someone we need to have rapport without friendship. Once we become friends with someone, we are usually too invested in the relationship to be friends with them to be able to coach them objectively. Try coaching your husband, wife, partner, kids or friends if you don't believe me. So how can we have rapport without friendship? Well, one of the things that we can do is employ some of the techniques from NLP (Neuro-linguistic Programming). These techniques can help us find an energetic connection with people without needing to be friends.

MIRRORING THE EMOTION OF THE COACHEE

Mirroring is a technique to build rapport with someone by subtly imitating their emotions through body language, tone of voice and word choice.[3] It works on the basic premise that people like people who are like themselves. For example, if a coachee is highly energetic and enthusiastic, perhaps speaking quickly, the coach can mirror this approach. Alternatively, if the coachee is more reserved or contemplative, perhaps speaking slowly and reservedly, the manager can mirror this style. This technique helps to build a sense of empathy, which in turn can make the coachee feel connected to their manager without being friends. However, it is crucial that the manager does this subtly to avoid seeming insincere or patronising.

PACING AND LEADING

Pacing and leading involves mirroring the emotions of the coachee as stated above and then leading them into a more reflective mindset. The idea is that once rapport is established, the manager can lead the conversation to a more reflective or productive state.[4] For example, if a team member speaks quickly and expresses frustration, the manager can match this style at first to build connection. Gradually, they can slow the pace and lead the coachee into a more reflective and open-minded space.

Using Reflective Listening

Reflective listening is a technique that can also build rapport. It involves using the words that a coachee says and essentially repeating them back to the coachee. This might extend to paraphrasing or summarising (sometimes called bottom lining) a coachee's thoughts and feelings. By showing that they are engaged in the conversation, the manager sends us a subconscious message that the coachee is important and worth listening to (remember *status* in SCARF). This technique fosters a sense of understanding and support without necessarily being friends.

Maintaining Boundaries

Not an NLP technique, but maintaining personal boundaries is crucial for managers. Managers should avoid sharing too much personal information at the risk of breaking rapport. There is a risk that the more we know about someone the more we might potentially dislike them. Too much small talk may potentially derail the purpose of the conversation, and the coaching session might lose its momentum.

It is important to remember that rapport can be achieved without being friends. Most people have experienced moments of connection with people they would not regard as friends. Furthermore, although rapport is important, coaching conversations are not meant to be all fun and light. There may be times where the coach asks challenging questions and 'the work' that needs to be done may at times be difficult.

The GROW Model

Sir John Whitmore's GROW model is probably the most well-known coaching framework.[5] It is a great tool that managers can leverage to help drive results and is solution focused. The model is really a loose structure that managers can follow so that their conversations move towards a solution. It stands for goal, reality, options and will (sometimes referred to as the 'way forward'). Here's how it works:

> **Goal:** At this stage the manager helps the coach define what they want to achieve from the session. They might tie this to a larger goal and question the reason that the coachee values the goal. This step ensures the conversation has a clear purpose. The manager might ask what a successful conversation would look like to help envisage the measures of success.
>
> **Reality:** Having explored the goal, the manager can then move onto assess the coachee's current situation, identifying challenges and attempting to understand the context. The manager might ask the coachee how far they currently are from their goal and what approaches they have already tried.

Options: After understanding the current situation, the manager helps the coachee to brainstorm solutions to the problem. The manager encourages the coachee to be creative and generate ideas without judgement. The manager might ask hypothetical questions here to stimulate more imaginative thinking and challenge assumptions.

Will: The final step is about commitment and action. The coach helps the coachee choose the best options from the list that they brainstormed previously. Together they try to make a concrete timeline of action and consider the support that the coachee may need. They should also discuss who will hold the coachee accountable – bear in mind this does not need to be the manager.

The GROW model stays rooted in being solution focused but allows the manager opportunities to dig deeper. The final stage allows a concrete path ahead, which ensures that there are tangible takeaways after conversations. However, it is important to note that managers should not pressure themselves into finding solutions. The moment they do, they might find themselves leading the conversation towards their own solutions. Furthermore, the GROW framework should not be followed in a dogmatic way. Conversations may move backwards and forwards as the conversation develops. Coaches should stay focused on the conversation rather than simply finish the conversation like an automation.

Example GROW-model Conversation

Let's take a look at Sofia modelling the GROW model in a non-directive conversation with her direct report – Jason Tan.

Goal

Sofia: So, what would you like to discuss in today's session Jason?

Jason: I would like to discuss how I can be more visible at work. Like . . . make my presence known in the organisation.

Sofia: What is the reason that this is important for you?

Jason: Well . . . I feel like people don't really know me outside this team. I think it might be affecting my opportunities for growth and even promotion.

Sofia: . . . right. So, what would a successful conversation look like for you today?

Jason: Maybe we can come up with some suggestions for how I can be more visible outside my team.

Sofia: Does this connect to any bigger goals that you have?

Jason: Well . . . I guess overall I want to grow in the bank and kind of unlock more opportunities for myself.

Reality

Sofia: So, how visible would you say you are now?

JASON: I don't think people really know me . . . for example, Jenny from transaction banking. Everyone knows her and she's in the same calls as me.

SOFIA: What is it that Jenny does which is different to you?

JASON: Hmmm . . . good question. I guess that she speaks out more on the calls . . . you know, even when she's not asking a great question. She makes sure her voice is heard, you know.

Options

Sofia: Is that something that you could perhaps try?

JASON: Well . . . yes, I could do that . . . maybe ask a question on one of our big calls . . . you know where senior leaders are on the call.

SOFIA: Is there anything else you could do?

JASON: Actually, yes . . . I remember you asking about a cross-functional team that would involve working with different parts of the business.

SOFIA: Yes, that's right. Do you think that would give you the visibility that you are looking for?

JASON: Maybe . . . but I guess not so much with senior leaders.

SOFIA: Is there anything else you could do?

JASON: Well . . .

After sharing more ideas . . .

Will

Sofia: So, what do you think is your best option?

Jason: I still think that speaking up on one of the bigger calls might give me the exposure that I need.

Sofia: Great. So, what is the first step that you can take towards doing this?

Jason: I need to find out when the next big call is and . . . prepare the right question to ask.

Sofia: Will you need anyone's support to do this?

Jason: Well . . . I was thinking that in our next conversation, you could help me prepare. What do you think?

Sofia: Yes . . . sure. We can do that. Let's reconnect next month to discuss this. Are you ok if we stop our session here?

Of course this shows a very accelerated conversation. In the full version, Sofia would go deeper into Jason's beliefs. She would probably ask what is holding Jason back from asking a question in the call. Usually, coaching conversations don't have simple solutions. If they did, we wouldn't need a coach!

Non-Directive Coaching and Therapy

Some people who are new to coaching might be tempted to think that coaching and therapy are the same. Both involve listening and asking questions, but they *are* fundamentally different. Coaching, as we saw in the GROW model, focuses on solutions. It may go back at times or dig deeper into the reasons behind an obstacle or blockage. However, it will rarely keep digging until it reaches the 'root cause'. This root cause may often be some trauma or deeply imbedded belief in the coachee's mind. To reach closure on this, the coachee may need therapy in order to move on. A coach is not a trained therapist and should resist the urge to try to 'cure' their coachee. Instead, they might ask a coachee sensitively if they are open to speaking to a therapist and suggest one in their professional network. Nowadays, much of the stigma surrounding therapy has been reduced as people recognise its value in promoting growth and well-being.

Imagine if a coachee needs to be assertive to progress at work. The coach stays solution focused but continually comes up against a blockage. There is a deep-seated fear in the coachee of aggressive people stemming from a childhood trauma of being bullied at school. As a result, the coachee continually adopts passive behaviour and avoids conflict or accommodates the other party. In this situation, the coach may need to suggest therapy for the coachee to help them overcome that trauma. Of course, the decision to accept therapy lies within the coachee and this should never be forced upon them.

Common New Coach Errors

New managers face a steep learning curve when it comes to adopting a non-directive approach to coaching. There are a few common mistakes that managers or indeed anyone new to coaching might make.

First, managers who have not exorcised their Theory X demons or who want to demonstrate their expertise to their coachee may fall into the mistake of giving advice. As mentioned before, this can limit the coachee's ability to grow and may lead to a dependency on solutions from the coach. The coachee may even resent the manager for assuming a position of 'knowing better' than the coachee.

Secondly, managers who are new to coaching may unintentionally lead conversations. They may steer discussions towards their own solutions or perspectives, unwittingly removing the coachee's chance to find their own solutions. This can have the impact of making the coachee feel less valued or heard and consequently impact trust.

Fear of silences or awkward pauses can also affect managers who are new to coaching. New managers may feel uncomfortable with silences or pauses and may attempt to fill these pauses with conversation out of fear of awkwardness. As a result, the coachee loses all-important moments of reflection. The pauses can be critical for a coachee to process information and make their own insights.

Another common error is that managers may overly focus on finding immediate solutions rather than digging for more long-term sustainable solutions. They may do this to prove to the coachee that they can bring value to a conversation and demonstrate their expertise or wisdom. The risk of this is that the approach can lead to superficial fixes rather than sustainable solutions.

Finally, new managers may panic when it comes to asking questions. They might become overfocused on asking seemingly challenging questions and by doing so accidentally stop staying present in the conversation. As the conversation moves, a question in the mind of the coach may lose its relevance and so managers must get used to abandoning questions and not being overly attached to any question they think of.

By recognising these common errors, new managers can try to develop a more effective coaching style that fosters deeper engagement, encourages critical thinking and supports their team's overall development.

Chapter Echo

Rupert stares at the screen displaying the stocks and shares in real time, the numbers and charts blinking out their chaotic rhythm.

Rhythm. Boom, boom, boom. What was it the doctor has called his heart condition? Left ventricular hypertrophy. That was it. The stress, the late nights, too many whiskies. They had taken their toll. But he hadn't listened. The doctor, his wife, even Bernard. They had all told him he was on his way to an early heart attack. What would it take him to change . . .?

Key Takeaways – Chapter Eight

1. Coaching as the Fifth Element

- Coaching is a unique and powerful method of empowerment, focusing on helping individuals realise their potential and foster personal growth.

- Coaching is specifically aimed at employees who have the potential and desire to achieve their goals.

- These conversations are motivational and challenging, aiming to help employees envision future successes, build confidence, step outside comfort zones and develop new skills and perspectives.

2. **Pros and Cons of a Directive Approach**

- Provides immediate solutions and clear steps, enhancing short-term efficiency and maintaining the manager's expert status.

- Can create dependency, limit ownership, lead to misalignment of solutions and inhibit long-term growth by hindering the development of problem-solving skills.

3. **Pros and Cons of a Non-Directive Approach**

- Encourages employees to take responsibility for their solutions, fostering personal growth and confidence. Builds resilience and critical thinking skills, ultimately benefiting long-term development.

- Can be challenging and time-consuming.

4. **Starting a Coaching Relationship**

- **Explain non-directive coaching:** Managers should clearly outline the principles of non-directive coaching, emphasising that the focus is on guiding employees to find their own solutions, which fosters personal growth and empowerment.

- **Clarify roles:** It's essential to delineate the roles within the coaching relationship, with managers serving as facilitators who ask open-ended questions and provide support, while coachees engage in self-reflection and take ownership of their development.

- **Address concerns:** Managers should acknowledge any apprehensions coachees may have about non-directive coaching, reassuring them that initial discomfort is part of the growth process and that support will be provided throughout.

- **Set clear goals and metrics:** Managers should outline collaboratively set goals and milestones, along with regular feedback sessions to track development, ensuring coachees understand how their efforts will be evaluated.

- **Motivation and focus:** By establishing clear expectations and support structures, managers can help coachees remain motivated and engaged in their development journey.

5. **Importance of Trust**

- **Emphasise confidentiality:** Managers should assure coachees that discussions will remain private, fostering a safe space for open communication.

- **Prioritise coaching sessions:** Scheduling regular sessions and treating them as important appointments demonstrates commitment, reinforcing the coachee's value.

- **Active listening:** Managers should engage fully, maintaining eye contact and responding thoughtfully, which helps build a supportive relationship.

- **Follow through on commitments:** Consistently delivering on promises made during sessions reinforces trust and credibility.

- **Fostering growth:** Building trust is essential for creating a productive coaching environment that supports coachee development.

6. Rapport without Friendship

- **Mirroring emotions:** Subtly reflecting the coachee's emotional state helps create empathy and understanding.

- **Pacing and leading:** Matching the coachee's communication style initially establishes rapport, after which managers can guide the conversation to a more reflective state.

- **Reflective listening:** Paraphrasing and summarising the coachee's thoughts validate their feelings and enhance engagement.

- **Maintain professional boundaries:** Managers should create a trusting environment while keeping the focus on professional development, avoiding overly familiar interactions.

7. GROW for Coaching

- **Structure of coaching:** The GROW model provides a framework for coaching sessions, focusing on four key elements: Goals, Reality, Options and Will.

- **Goals:** The first step is to set clear and achievable goals, giving direction and purpose to the coaching conversation.

- **Reality:** This phase involves assessing the coachee's current situation, identifying challenges and gaining clarity about their present context.

- **Options:** Coachees brainstorm potential strategies to achieve their goals, fostering creative thinking and empowering them to explore various possibilities.

- **Will:** The final step focuses on commitment, where the coach helps the coachee develop a concrete action plan, including specific actions and accountability measures.

8. Coaching and Therapy

- **Distinction between coaching and therapy:** Coaching focuses on performance enhancement and goal-setting, while therapy addresses emotional and psychological issues, often exploring past experiences.

- **Sensitive recommendations:** Managers should gently suggest therapy when significant emotional barriers hinder progress, framing it as an additional resource rather than a critique.

9. Common Errors by New Coaches

- **Providing solutions:** New managers may offer direct solutions to appear knowledgeable, which can hinder coachee growth and create dependency.

- **Leading conversations:** Unintentionally steering discussions can reduce the coachee's opportunity to express themselves, impacting trust and rapport.

- **Fear of silence:** Avoiding pauses can prevent critical reflection, which is essential for coachees to process information and gain insights.

- **Rushing for solutions:** Focusing on immediate fixes can overshadow deeper exploration of challenges, leading to superficial outcomes.

- **Anxiety about questioning:** Hesitance to ask questions can disrupt the flow of conversation and limit meaningful exploration of the coachee's needs.

Reflection Questions

- Do you like to receive advice from others? Why/ why not?

- What is an important life lesson you learned yourself? What triggered you to learn it?

INFLUENCE

Influence is our inner ability to lift people up to our perspective.

—Joseph Wong

REFLECTION TASK: INFLUENCE

Statement	Strongly Disagree (1)	Disagree (2)	Neutral (3)	Agree (4)	Strongly Agree (5)
1. I build rapport with my team members to establish trust and credibility.					
2. I frequently use my authority to enforce decisions.					
3. I use storytelling to convey important messages and inspire my team.					
4. I rely on formal power to get things done.					
5. I seek input and feedback from my team to shape decisions.					
6. I often remind my team of my position to assert control.					
7. I lead by example to influence my team's behaviour.					
8. I use my position to dominate discussions.					

Statement	Strongly Disagree (1)	Disagree (2)	Neutral (3)	Agree (4)	Strongly Agree (5)
9. I encourage collaboration and collective problem-solving.					
10. I use my position to resolve conflicts rather than facilitating dialogue.					

Read the chapter before you check your answers on pp. 266–267

The Need for Influence

As organisations change and become flatter and more agile, managers are increasingly less able to rely on position or knowledge power. This necessitates a more nuanced approach to leadership where leaders must utilise a powerful tool: influence. This powerful tool can help managers to inspire, motivate and engage teams without relying on the traditional threats and rewards system.

Research would suggest that younger generations are increasingly less likely to respect authority, solely based on position power.[1] They seek visionary leaders who can connect empathetically with them and foster deeper connections. This generational shift underscores the need for leaders to be able to lift and use the power of influence to achieve goals.

To cultivate their skills of influence, managers must work on their ability to actively listen, persuade others and develop their emotional intelligence. Managers can ensure that they can relate team goals with the broader organisational vision that can help develop a sense of shared purpose.

As managers navigate this new era of leadership, the ability to influence without reliance on position, rewards or threats is critical. By embracing influence as an essential competency, managers can create a culture of trust, collaboration and shared achievement that can, in turn, lead to more engaged teams.

Influence is a big word, and many managers and leaders will understand it differently. As we return to Mango Bank, let's explore how Kelly and Sofia influence others and discover the impact of the approach each manager uses.

KELLY

At Mango Bank, Kelly relies heavily on traditional position power to get things done. Once, during a project update discussion, she noticed that a critical task was behind schedule. Kelly, honing the responsible persons in her sights, opened fire with a round of threats. 'You are supposed to meet deadlines. That's why we have them. If you are unable to deliver on time, there will be consequences.' 'Like what, afternoon detention?' one of the braver new recruits quipped under their breath. Kelly, immune to humour, continued her steadfast tone, emphasising control over collaboration.

This approach did the opposite of fostering a sense of ownership. Instead, Kelly's approach led to a simmering culture of fear in which team members were expected to complete tasks without asking that all-important word 'why'. The team knew that questioning tasks could results in a one-way ticket to the 'Danger Zone', also referred to as Kelly's office.

As time passed, Kelly's reliance on positional power started to create fractures in the team. Some team members complied, enjoying the sense of order and being told what to do. Others started to feel disengaged, feeling more like extras in a cheap soap opera than valuable team members. Team members became creative at avoiding Kelly's wrath and dodging bullets rather than brainstorming creative ideas or challenging the status quo.

Once, Kelly gathered her team for a brainstorming session in one of the banks grander meeting rooms. 'I want us to think outside the box', Kelly had declared. 'Just as long as it's not too far' one of the bolder souls had whispered.

In the end, the approach started to leave Kelly feeling isolated. As she became more insecure, she clung to this position power further, whispering to herself that she needed to keep people in check. The changes Kelly needed to make were as obvious as a typo in a PowerPoint slide: easily fixable but only if someone would call them out.

And so, Kelly continues, her behaviour dictated by the beliefs that she's doing things the only way they can be done.

SOFIA

Sofia follows an approach which emphasises building relationships and cultivating a collaborative environment. For example, during a recent team meeting, instead of delivering a tirade of directives, Sofia began the meeting with a fun story about a time when her team, faced with a challenging project timeline, had worked closely to achieve incredible results.

'Remember that time we thought we'd be buried under an avalanche of documents and forms? Well, we managed to turn that avalanche into our own ice-skating rink!' Sofia chortled, setting off people laughing in the meeting room and immediately helping to thaw any anxiety or tension.

When discussing a new project or initiative, Sofia always invites input from her team. 'I'd love to hear your thoughts on how we might approach this', she would ask. She would frame conversations around her team's knowledge and expertise which would make them feel valued and engaged.

When she needs to persuade, Sofia combines a mixture of emotional appeal with logical reasoning. This balance helps her appeal to different team members, from the most process-oriented to the more people-driven communicators.

When faced with challenges, Sofia rarely resorts to the 'because I'm telling you to do it' approach. Instead, she encourages her team to come up with solutions, helping everyone to feel involved in the decision-making process.

Through her storytelling, charm, charisma and emotional intelligence, Sofia transforms her workplace culture. She builds an environment where people feel safe to share ideas, take risks and even innovate. As a result, Sofia's influence isn't just about authority, it's about connection and inspiration. It's about lifting others.

DEFINING INFLUENCE

Influence is defined by Tim Baker, one of the foremost experts on influence, as 'the power to make other people agree with your opinions or get them to do what you want, willingly and ethically'.[2] So, influence is perhaps a combination of using both power and persuasion. But what is power?

Influence and Power

There are different types of power as opposed to just position power. These types of power account for shifting dynamics even within hierarchical organisations.[3] Let's explore these seven types of power together:

1. **Legitimate power**

   This is the power a manager wields by virtue of being higher in the hierarchy than others. This power enables them to make decisions and give orders. The higher someone is in the hierarchy, the more power they have over others.

2. Coercive power

This is the power to make others compliant through fear of punishment. This might include threats of disciplinary action, being demoted or even fired. Coercive power might work in the short term but can lead to long-term resentment and toxicity.

3. Reward power

This is the ability to offer incentives like bonuses, benefits and promotions to encourage others to be compliant. Managers can motivate their teams by using rewards for certain behaviour. Rewards can involve both hygiene factors (monetary reward) and motivators (recognition, achievement).

4. Referent power

This is the charm or leadership qualities that a manager possesses. Referent power depends on how much the team members admire and respect the manager. This type of power is built on trust and loyalty. There is nothing for the follower to gain from referent power other than strengthening bonds with their manager.

5. Expert power

Obviously, this is related to the knowledge and expertise someone may have in a particular field. When someone is seen as an expert, others are likely to follow their advice and recommendations. In modern teams, expert power is distributed between the manager and other experts.

6. Information power

This type of power stems from having access to information that others might not have. This might be knowledge of organisational dynamics or strategic insights that others do not have access to. People with information power can sway decision-making with this knowledge.

7. Connection power

It's not what you know, it's who you know. Connection power points to a person's ability to draw on other powerful connections to give themselves power. This might involve being close to leaders inside or outside an organisation and leveraging them for power or resources.

KELLY'S TOXIC INFLUENCE

At Mango Bank, Kelly primarily relies on legitimate, coercive, reward and information power to influence her team. Her legitimate power comes from her seniority at Mango Bank, and she uses this power to try to ensure compliance. When team members fall short, Kelly resorts to coercive power and issues threats of punishments to try to initiate improved performance. This approach succeeds in jumpstarting the team's engine momentarily but does not address the engine itself — which is not being fuelled correctly. Anyway, enough about engines!

When team members perform, Kelly utilises reward power focused on achieving targets. These rewards offer short-term incentives but do not help build any loyalty in the team. Often, they foster individual competition and feuds as team members vie to stay in Kelly's good books.

Kelly, like many managers, uses information power by controlling access to crucial data and knowledge of what is happening higher up in the organisation. Kelly keeps critical information to herself or shares it only with her closest confidants. This helps her to maintain control and she can reward others by giving them privilege to such secret information. Unfortunately, this creates a sense of alienation in her team who feel like they are being withheld important information. Murmurs and gossip fill the void left by the lack of communication.

Sofia's Empowering Influence

Sofia's approach leverages referent power. This is rooted in her outstanding ability to build strong and trusting relationships with her team members. She makes herself approachable, empathetic and persuasive, all of which encourage her team members to follow her willingly. Her relational approach helps to create a culture of mutual respect and loyalty.

Sofia's style contrasts with Kelly's as she emphasises influence through connection rather than control. People follow Sofia, not out of fear, but out of loyalty and respect. Of course, Sofia does use the other levers of power at times. For example, she uses expert power when she shares her knowledge of skills to direct her team members. She might use connection power when she wants to help connect her team to fulfil a task or to help them grow.

Nevertheless, Sofia's main tool is referent power. As she focuses on building trust and rapport, when she does use other levers of power, they are seen as empowering rather than controlling.

PERSUASION AND EMOTION

We can persuade people with appeals to both emotion and logic. Logical persuasion often involves the presentation of factual and quantitative information to influence an audience. It is the reliance on data to drive decision-making. However, there is increasing evidence to suggest that a large part of decision-making is influenced by emotions rather than logic. This has been highlighted by the work of psychologists Daniel Kahneman and Amos Tversky[4] as well as by the neuroscientist Antonio Damasio.[5] It is therefore essential that leaders who aim to lift others are adept at influencing others through emotional persuasion. This does not mean manipulation before you ask! Managers who choose the leadership route persuade others for collective benefits without any treacherous end goal.

STORY AND INFLUENCE

One of the most powerful tools of influence is story. Why is story so powerful? Well, stories when told correctly connect with the audience at an emotional level. This in turn makes them more memorable and things which we remember are easier to apply (remember Bloom's Taxonomy? You don't ... I should have used a story). As stories activate different parts of the brain, like sensory experiences and emotions, they can also help people overcome objections. As people become more involved in a narrative, they may overcome a knee-jerk response to the information that is presented. For example, if information that someone shares contradicts a belief an audience member has, they will be likely to reject that message outright. A story can help shift that person's attention to the unfolding of the story through suspense and emotional investment. Storytelling can also help as a non-directive tool that forces the listener to reflect deeply and infer their own meaning.

Effective managers tell stories. As time passes, these stories are often communicated throughout the organisation and help become the fabric of organisational culture. I have woven several stories into this book to help you remember their truths.

Sofia's Story of Change

Sofia stood, arms by her side at the front of the conference room. She could feel the scepticism in the room swirling around like the dense mist she remembers falling off the hills in her Malaysian hometown. Mango Bank had announced significant restructuring, and her team were anxious about the changes and their implications. Sofia realised that if she openly tried to 'sell the change', her team might perceive her as the voice from the top. The voice of Sauron perhaps. As a result, Sofia decided to tell a story.

Good morning, everyone. I understand that the news of the restructuring has left some of you feeling slightly uneasy. I can completely relate because I have been there myself. Let me take you back to a few years ago when I was working with my previous company.

At that time, I was leading a small and dynamic team. Very similar to you guys. We had a solid routine and a great workflow. Everything was going great until one day we received news from our manager at the time that we were going to receive a new project management tool that would radically overhaul how we worked. I remember thinking to myself, I love the old system. It was familiar and reliable. The new system seemed complicated and unnecessary. I was resistant and I didn't hesitate to voice my concerns.

Despite my resistance the change was going to happen. We had a series of training sessions, and it was a really steep learning curve. I remember many late nights trying to figure out the system and wondering deep down if all of this made sense.

Just as I was at my wits end, something amazing started to happen.

Sofia paused and looked at her audience. Scanning their faces. Everyone was focused on her.

I started to realise that the new system cut out loads of extra work. It also helped us track projects better, improved communication and gave us powerful insights that we had never even thought about. Slowly we managed to increase our productivity, and our team was collaborating like never before.

A real pivotal moment came when a feature in the new system helped us identify problems before they even occurred. We delivered the project way ahead of schedule and received some amazing feedback from our client. The new system had helped us to evolve and adapt. To become better at what we do.

I learned a powerful lesson through that experience. Change can be daunting and it's only natural for us to resist it. But if we persevere and give change a chance it can help us discover strengths and abilities that we didn't know we had.

As Sofia finished her story, she could sense a change in the energy of the room. The cloud of scepticism had parted and given way to a ray of quiet optimism and curiosity. Sofia's story had resonated with her team, and they would remember it on their bumpy journey through the change.

A Manager's Story Toolkit

Of course, Sofia hadn't made that story up on the spot. She had taken it from her mental toolkit. A place where she had loosely memorised several stories that she could pull out and tell convincingly. These stories gave her team an understanding of her journey as a manager as well as illustrations of her character; all of which helped to build her sense of connection and trust with her team.

A great toolkit contains a range of stories that can be used at different moments.[6] A manager should have stories of success that they can use to highlight their competence and leadership capabilities. However, it is also important for managers to share stories of setback or failure. These can be powerful ways for managers to show their vulnerability and illustrate how we can grow from failure. They can help to develop a culture where failure is reframed as learning.

As well as stories of success and failure, influential managers should be able to share stories of change. These stories can help showcase the bumpiness of change and help team members accept that there are benefits. This can help ease tensions and potentially reduce resistance.

Additionally, managers should have stories of conflict at hand. These stories can help explore how conflicts were resolved and these can be used to illustrate the importance of collaboration, empathy and problem-solving. These stories can provide insights into how conflicts can be springboards to closer collaboration and improved understanding.

By sharing their stories, managers enhance their authenticity, relatability and credibility. They also empower their teams to embrace challenges, adapt to change and navigate conflict effectively.

Real vs Fictional Stories

Should all stories be real? Not necessarily. A fictional story can illustrate a powerful truth. Just think of 'Little Red Riding Hood' or 'The Boy Who Cried Wolf'.

However, stories that are real tend to resonate with the storyteller more. This can help the manager tell the story more convincingly. When a storyteller is emotionally invested in the story, it would make sense that the audience are too.

STORYTELLING INGREDIENTS

Great stories often rely on their ability to generate suspense in the listener. This suspense captures the audience's attention and keeps them engaged as they try to anticipate what will happen next. This anticipation creates a sense of focus. This heightened attention is due to the release of dopamine in the brain, a neurotransmitter associated with pleasure and reward that elevates memory and learning.[7] Remember we said that stories are more memorable!

To build suspense, storytellers can employ different stages in their story that signify change. They can use pauses at crucial points in the story so that their audience rush ahead, anticipating what will happen. They can increase the pace of their story to increase excitement or slow down to build focus.

In addition to suspense, empathy is a vital ingredient for a successful story. When the audience feels a connection with the storyteller, they are more likely to become emotionally invested in the story. This connection is facilitated by the release of another hormone: oxytocin. Also known as the 'love hormone' oxytocin is linked to building trust and bonding between people. By harnessing empathy, managers can help build a sense of trust in their listener.[8] Managers can leverage empathy by making themselves and their emotional state relatable in their stories.

Alternatively, a good story is also free from over-explanation and jargon. It should not rely on establishing expertise through complex language or use of data. These can force the audience back into their normal thinking patterns and potentially spoil the effects of the story. Imagine being given a 10-minute interlude about how the Death Star functions in the middle of a Star Wars episode! A good story must instead be clear, concise and relatable without forcing the audience to get bogged down in too much information.

When we tell a story, we may want to clearly articulate the learning point to our audience. This is because different audiences may read different meanings into different stories. This can bridge the story to the current context and help switch from story mode back into the real situation at hand.

The Story of Stories

In Persia, there once lived a powerful king Shahryar. He had become embittered about love and fidelity and decided to marry a new woman every day, only to have her executed the next morning.

One day, a brave and smart young lady named Scheherazade volunteered to become the King's bride. Everyone who knew her was terrified about what would happen.

On the first evening of their marriage, Scheherazade told the King a wonderful story, filled with adventure. The King was enthralled by the story and didn't say a word. As dawn approached, Scheherazade paused the story at a critical point, promising him that she would finish the story the following evening. The King spared her life if she continued the story.

The next evening, Scheherazade finished the story and began to spin another enchanting tale. Again, the King spared her life.

On and on this continued, for 1,001 nights until eventually the King had fallen hopelessly in love with Scheherazade. She had taught him to trust and love again.

Chapter Echo

Rupert settled back into his chair. His favourite part of the day was late afternoon. The urgency of the morning was past, and his energy levels were still high. He had just finished his mentoring session with one of the Bank's leaders, Alvin Lim. He had asked Rupert, 'how can I have more influence' in the Bank. Rupert had responded, 'It's not what you know, it's who you know, Alvin.' As the afternoon sun cast shadows over his office table, he reflected on whether he agreed with his own suggestion or if he even liked it.

Key Takeaways – Chapter Nine

1. The Need for Influence

- **Shift in leadership dynamics:** Traditional power structures are evolving, and managers often find themselves with diminished positional or knowledge power, making influence a critical skill.

- **Generational changes:** Younger generations seek leaders who can connect on a deeper level, demonstrating empathy and providing a compelling vision rather than relying solely on authority.

- **Skills for effective influence:** Managers must develop skills like active listening, emotional intelligence and persuasive communication to inspire and engage their teams without relying on threats or rewards.

2. Types of Power

- **Legitimate power:** Authority from a formal position.

- **Coercive power:** Influence through fear of punishment.

- **Reward power:** Influence through incentives.

- **Referent power:** Influence through personal qualities and charisma.

- **Expert power:** Influence through knowledge and skills.

- **Information power:** Influence through access to valuable information.

3. Persuasion and Emotion

- **Importance of emotions:** Emotions play a significant role in decision-making, often more than logic.

- **Storytelling:** Effective storytelling connects on an emotional level, making the message memorable and helping to overcome objections. It serves as a non-directive tool for personal reflection.

4. A Manager's Story Toolkit

- **Diverse stories:** Managers should have stories of success, failure, change and conflict to connect with their team and foster a sense of trust and understanding.

- **Purpose of stories:** Stories of success inspire, stories of failure humanise the manager, stories of change influence during transitions and stories of conflict illustrate constructive resolution.

5. Storytelling Ingredients

- **Building suspense:** Change creates suspense, capturing attention and enhancing memory through dopamine release.

- **Empathy:** Sharing personal anecdotes and relatable characters fosters empathy and trust through oxytocin release.

- **Avoid Over-Explanation:** Keeping stories clear and relatable avoids diminishing their emotional impact and ensures engagement.

Reflection Questions

- What Is a story you remember from your childhood? Why do you remember it?

- How often do you tell stories at work?

THINKING BIG

Tomorrow belongs to those who can hear it coming.

—David Bowie

REFLECTION TASK: BIG-PICTURE THINKING CHECKER FOR MANAGERS

Please rate each statement based on how much you agree with it:

Statement	Strongly Disagree (1)	Disagree (2)	Neutral (3)	Agree (4)	Strongly Agree (5)
1. You enjoy routine and repetitious tasks.					
2. You like to talk to your friends about new ideas you have.					
3. You can give examples of initiatives happening in other departments within your organisation.					
4. You sometimes can't sleep trying to solve a problem.					
5. People see you as more of a doer than a talker.					
6. You rarely have new ideas that you want to share.					
7. You are generally optimistic.					
8. You are usually suspicious of change.					
9. You see the future as more of a threat than an opportunity.					
10. You rarely multitask and prefer to do things in a linear order.					

Statement	Strongly Disagree (1)	Disagree (2)	Neutral (3)	Agree (4)	Strongly Agree (5)
11. When you are given a new task to do you focus on the process rather than the result.					
12. You believe that if you can take care of the details the rest will take care of itself.					
13. You are good at seeing patterns in unconnected things.					
14. You spend time imagining your future.					
15. People might describe you as spontaneous or even chaotic.					
16. When someone shares an idea, you immediately question how practical it is.					
17. You tend to make mistakes with routine work.					
18. After a meeting you can usually remember many details clearly.					
19. You love brainstorming and creative thinking sessions.					
20. You are easily bored by familiarity.					

Read the chapter before you check your answers on pp. 265–269

The Big Picture

Managers who empower their people are often left wondering what they should do with their new-found freedom aside from people management. Well, this shift allows them time to focus on more strategic tasks. By freeing up their schedule from BAU focus and detail-oriented work, managers can have a chance to do some dreaming. Remember Sofia, staring into space and sipping jasmine tea? That's her doing some dreaming and thinking of the big picture.

The big picture doesn't just mean looking outside the team silo. It in fact refers to looking beyond daily operational concerns and exploring future trends, innovative strategies and potential disruptors. This broader perspective is crucial for anticipating future challenges and opportunities that might not be evident when a manager is knee deep in the minutiae of daily operations. Managers who focus excessively on BAU risk missing important industrial shifts or emerging innovations.

If managers can empower their team to handle routine tasks and decision-making, they can spend more time on this big-picture thinking. Managers who engage with the bigger picture are more likely to steer their organisations through change and remain competitive. Considering the big picture may not have the frenetic energy of the BAU as it involves deeper reflection and thinking. As a result, some managers will steer clear of it, preferring to have their time devoured by what they know rather than what could be.

Let's step back inside the halls of Mango Bank to see how Kelly and Sofia manage their big-picture thinking.

KELLY

At Mango Bank, Kelly bustles through the corridors like a mini tornado. She's deeply focused on details and BAU tasks, driven by a need to remain in control and ensure efficiency. Her calendar is a colourful forest, filled with meetings and discussions that cover every aspect and contingency of daily operations.

This fixation on control and intricacies means that Kelly is often slow to adopt more innovative practices. For example, Kelly's team lag behind Mango Bank's competitors in terms of client onboarding. Other banks have adopted fast, seamless processes whilst Kelly's team still lag behind using legacy approaches with multiple touchpoints. Meetings to discuss enhancing onboarding might even end up with Kelly agonising over tiny points like the position of the company brand in automated emails. This obsessive attention to detail, whilst vital at the execution stage, often leads to missed opportunities for Kelly's team and Mango Bank as a whole.

Kelly's resistance to delegate and her preoccupation with all aspects of the team's tasks generates a bottleneck. Her capable team feel constrained by the bureaucracy of her approach and disempowered to take risks or even small decisions. As a result, Mango Bank struggles to keep up with competitors who have adopted more agile approaches.

Kelly is lauded for her metrics, which speak volumes of efficiency and error reduction. However, disruptive ideas are less common than a square pineapple in an electric wheelbarrow. As Kelly is maxed out chasing the latest efficiency-driven goal, there is rarely even time for her to savour the taste of her favourite Hokkien Mee.

SOFIA

Sofia often dreams about the future. You can sometimes see her eyes slightly glazed, mouth open, thinking deeply. Sofia is thinking of the future but not in an anxious way. She spends significant time in her day reading extensively and exploring diverse industries. Her mind flits between ideas, rummaging around and looking for unusual connections.

Her predilection for unusual associations between ideas sometimes leads to remarkable and truly creative breakthroughs. One remarkable story sticks to mind. Once whilst reading about a hospital's revolutionary platform that could track patients in real time, Sofia had the idea of implementing this at Mango Bank. With her trademark optimism, Sofia pitched the idea to her team. She sold the team on the idea that it could enhance cross-departmental collaboration as well as reduce duplicated work and errors. Soon, other departments were catching on to Sofia's innovation and outside industry thinking.

Beyond her innovative ideas, Sofia also works hard to break down silos in the organisation. She can often be seen having lunch with an array of different teams, listening carefully with her blend of warm intensity. This broader, organisational perspective helps Sofia keep abreast of innovation happening throughoul Mango Bank as well as the challenges that other teams face. It creates a more holistic view of customer journeys and how each part of the jigsaw connects.

Sofia's ability to question processes and challenge expected norms help her to push boundaries. Her natural curiosity and growth mindset drive her to look for interesting solutions in unusual places. While Kelly's team remain stuck in the quagmire of BAU, Sofia's team are forging ahead, innovating and staying within touch of the industry's movers and shakers. Kelly's approach pays homage to the need for some slack both in her own daily work and her team. Sometimes creativity needs a little space to breathe for ideas to germinate. Those moments where ideas dance in our subconscious can be the perfect breeding ground for really disruptive concepts.

BIG-PICTURE THINKING

Big-picture thinking is a powerful set of techniques that managers can employ to zoom out from the details of day-to-day work and see a broader perspective. Picture a monkey in the forests of Malaysia, whose reality is defined by the trees and forest until one day it climbs a particularly tall tree and sees the fast-developing township on the fringes of its forest.

Big-picture thinking involves using a number of techniques like scanning the horizon and looking for emerging political, economic, social, technological, legal or environmental (PESTLE) trends. It also involves imagining the future by making connections between diverse ideas (synthesis), challenging assumptions and taking on different perspectives.

To develop our big-picture thinking acumen, we need to continuously grow and diversify our knowledge base, deepen our understanding and knowledge of our customers and let loose our creative ideas. It also involves looking to the future or futurism: using patterns in the past to help us to try to predict the future.

Big-picture thinking is a different mindset to BAU. It involves being playful and suspending judgement whilst being creative. It, of course, doesn't mean abandoning traditional approaches to strategy, which can leverage powerful insights. However, the difference is that big-picture thinking attempts to give us a vision of the future rather than a snapshot of the present. To do this, we might need to abandon analytical thinking and venture into the unknown.

The risk of not thinking big is that we might miss big opportunities. We become victims of the future rather than authors of it.

Of course, big-picture thinkers need to work closely with more detail-oriented people to translate their ideas into results. Big-picture thinkers must be able to communicate their ideas clearly and succinctly to different types of stakeholders whilst clearly articulating the risks of not changing. They need to be able to translate abstract visions into concrete plans with the help of their teams.

SCANNING THE HORIZON

Through PESTLE, managers can gain an understanding of the environment in which their business operates. This analysis helps managers identify potential opportunities and threats for their business. It forces managers to recognise the interdependence of different factors and how something seemingly disparate can be a complete game changer.

PESTLE, in more detail, stands for:

Political: This includes factors like government policies, political stability, tax policies, trade tariffs and regulations.

Economic: This explores factors like inflation, economic stability, inflation and exchange rates.

Social: This examines social trends and cultural changes.

Technological: This focuses on technological enhancements, automation and artificial intelligence.

Legal: This would encompass laws related to health and safety, employment and consumer protection.

Environmental: This would of course include environmental aspects like sustainability and environmental regulations.

ENVISIONING THE FUTURE WITH PESTLE

A PESTLE analysis is a powerful tool for surveying the current and emerging landscape. It is what BAU is built upon. To envision the future, managers can create short-, medium- and long-term futures. This approach is used by McKinsey in their three horizons strategy, which helps organisations with both the current situation and future possibilities.[1] The three horizons are as follows:

Horizon one: Focuses on the immediate term and explores how to optimise the status quo.

Horizon two: Identifies emerging opportunities and new growth areas.

Horizon three: Explores potential disruptors and transformative innovation.

Managers can apply the three horizons approach to a PESTLE analysis, looking at short-, medium- and long-term futures. This can help facilitate innovation at various degrees of disruption. Managers can even look at strategies that can potentially cover all three horizons: the sweet spot, if you like. The activity can help managers consider both short- and long-term visions of the future, moving from the known into the unknown.

Of course, managers wouldn't be expected to do these envisioning activities on their own. They might work best cross-functionally with different team members to leverage different perspectives and deeper levels of knowledge. Working with multiple minds can help overcome biases that might inhibit our ability to be disruptive as we might rely on overly familiar patterns.

FUTURE CUSTOMER PERSONAS

To help build disruptive ideas, managers can work on their empathy skills. A great way to do this, often in conjunction with a future-focused PESTLE, is to build a customer future persona. The persona is designed to represent a future customer segment, their beliefs and preferences. This is a fun way to see how an organisation can stay solution-focused: working on solving potential problems. A good persona should contain ideas on the person's: geographics (e.g., area), demographics (e.g., education), psychographics (e.g., personality) and any behavioural aspects or preferences a customer might have.[2]

The future persona can be a fun way of empathising with the customers of the future, influenced by the context of the future PESTLE. What will be the problems of the children of tomorrow and how can we serve them better?

Continuous Learning

Earlier we discussed the importance of the growth mindset. This is essentially continuous learning. Managers who want to find the bigger picture must continue to engage in key activities.

- **Reading widely:** Reading can help managers expand their knowledge base, which can in turn help them connect diverse ideas. Besides, reading can help managers develop creativity and imagination as well as reduce stress. Reading doesn't have to only be about boring management books (Ahem!) but anything that piques the reader's interest.

- **Networking externally and internally:** Engaging with experts both inside and outside the organisation can help develop a breeding ground for new ideas. This can help spark ideas that might not emerge from the isolation of the team or even the organisation. Many large organisations are so prone to silos that innovative ideas haven't even broken out of teams or departments.

- **Learning from outside the industry:** Exposure to different industries can help managers apply different ideas in new contexts (a bit like Sofia). Looking at innovation from different industries can provoke new ways of thinking.

CHALLENGING ASSUMPTIONS

Continuous learners don't take things at face value. They are constantly:

- **Critically evaluating:** They constantly challenge assumptions and well-held beliefs. They rethink the status quo, and their growth mindset drives the belief that things can be continuously improved and reinvented. This habit ensures that they never become complacent, resting on their laurels.

- **Encouraging diverse thinking:** Managers who think big are constantly encouraging different perspectives from different people. This can lead to increased conflict, but in a collaborative environment that Theory Y managers develop, conflict is seen as the stepping stone to breakthrough.

SYNTHESIS AND INNOVATION

If we remember, the final level of Bloom's Taxonomy was creativity or synthesis. This is the ability to connect ideas together to form new wholes. Not an easy feat. The power of synthesis can harness powerful results:

- **New markets:** Combining antithetical elements can create completely new markets and send ripples through an industry. For example, the combination of gaming and fitness led to the creation of Pokémon Go, which encouraged physical gaming through augmented reality. I'm sure you remember a time when everyone was playing that!

- **Disruption:** Combining unusual ideas can lead to disruption in an industry. Companies like Grab have revolutionised the taxi service by connecting it with smartphone technology. This has been a gamechanger in many countries and developed a whole gig economy.

- **Breakthrough ideas:** Where different industries meet, there are often breakthrough ideas. The connection of fitness and tech helped to shape the fitness tracker industry. Wearable technology and the internet of things have redefined health and fitness.

Practical Steps for Managers to Foster Synthesis

Synthesis seems like a challenging goal for anyone. You might be thinking, not everyone can generate breakthrough ideas that transform industries. Surely, this is reserved for a handful of geniuses who live off nitro coffee in a bunker somewhere. But actually, we are playing with new connections all the time in our brain. Managers can help develop their ability to make connections by:

Breaking things into different pieces: this could be products, services or processes. This is the analyse stage of Bloom's Taxonomy. Once we look at parts separately, we can evaluate their use and potentially remove or rearrange them. This can also help efficiency as Toyota discovered when they created their just-in-time system, which helped reduce waste.

Practising making unusual connections between things: In training, I have a fun activity that I run. It simply involves coming up with unusual connections between things, like Macha and Octopus! Once we are primed to look for these unusual connections, we might start to see connections in our business or outside.

Playing with ideas: Managers can play with ideas and encourage others to do the same. Once in a state of play, managers can help overcome the self-regulating thoughts that might stifle new ideas.

Avoiding overfocusing on originality: Sometimes, we may strive so hard for originality, we self-censor. This forces the brain back into critical thinking and limits our output. This is known as *cognitive rigidity*. In studies conducted, overfocusing on originality can paradoxically lead to this *phenomenon*, which actually leads to more rigid patterns of thinking.[3]

Changing states: I mean doing things that can access more subconscious thoughts. For example, we sometimes have breakthrough ideas when we have a shower or go for a jog. The process of neurogenesis demonstrates that new patterns are formed in the brain when we exercise. Finally, sleeping. Sleeping can help release powerful ideas especially during the REM (rapid eye movement) phase.[4] During this time, the brain can roam through concepts and memories freely, which can facilitate the emergence of powerful and unexpected ideas.

FUTURISM AND BIG DATA

The future is uncertain. Big data analytics involves exploring large data sets to uncover insights that can help inform decision-making. By examining big data, organisations can anticipate future trends, optimise operations and innovate their products and services. However, big data analytics has limited ability to predict human behaviour, which is subject to mysterious variables like emotion. One classic example of a company that overly relied on big data and familiar patterns was Nokia. They leveraged big data to optimise efficiency but did not pay enough attention to the fundamental shift that was happening in the industry towards smartphones. By the time they took stock of the situation, it was already too late.

There are three key lessons that managers can learn from the fate of Nokia:

Beyond data: Nokia's experience underlines the importance of looking outside data sets. While big data is a powerful tool for revealing current trends and optimising efficiency, it may not predict disruptive changes in human behaviour and preferences.

Human insight: Managers might need to combine quantitative data with more qualitative data. This can help account for the human element and provide insights into the beliefs and feelings people have. For example, complaints about a product or service give us an idea of changing expectations.

Agility and innovation: Organisations must remain agile and open to innovation. Managers must stay tuned to subtle shifts in the market and be prepared to use their voice in meetings to influence leaders to change or pivot their strategy.

THINKING BIG AND FEAR

When people are afraid, they tend to throw themselves back into the BAU as a source of comfort. By being focused on the road, we don't see the gaping cavern in front of us. Managers who remain steadfast in the BAU, may comfort themselves that they are working hard. But they may be putting off the more challenging thinking of envisioning the future. So, managers must remain brave, with their heads looking forwards. They must give themselves time to dream and not be sucked back into firefighting and detail focus.

Ultimately, how do we want to be remembered? For hitting our key performance indicators, ensuring the BAU runs smoothly, beating another metric? Or for genuine innovation and making the human experience better? For looking to the road or looking to the horizon?

Chapter Echo

As the sun begins to set in the Singapore sky and the city building lights wink in the gloaming, Rupert begins to pack his briefcase. Had he made the right decision about the MD post? Cynthia had certainly seemed a little unsure of his advice. Two women leaders applying for an MD post. Who would have thought? As he snips off his desk lamp, he feels a strange sense of pride . . . Mango Bank really had changed under his tenure. A flicker of light fills the office momentarily as Rupert closes the door and heads for the lift.

Key Takeaways – Chapter Ten

The Importance of Empowerment and Big Picture Thinking

1. **Empowerment frees time for strategic thinking:** Managers who delegate routine tasks can shift their focus to strategic activities, fostering long-term success.

2. **Big-picture thinking:** Involves looking beyond daily operations to consider long-term objectives, emerging trends and potential disruptions. This broader perspective helps anticipate future challenges and opportunities.

3. **Risk of BAU focus:** Managers overly focused on BAU tasks risk missing important industry shifts and innovations.

Fostering Innovation through Synthesis

1. **Combining antithetical ideas:** Innovation can stem from merging seemingly unrelated concepts. For example: The iPhone combined mobile communication and computing, revolutionising both industries.

2. **Practical steps:** Encourage diverse thinking, experiment with unlikely combinations, look beyond the industry and challenge assumptions to foster synthesis and innovation.

Strategic Tools and Frameworks

1. **PESTLE analysis:** Evaluates external macro-environmental factors (political, economic, social, technological, legal, environmental) to identify opportunities and threats.

2. **Three Horizons Framework (McKinsey):** Helps organisations manage current performance while exploring and preparing for future opportunities and disruptions:

   - Horizon 1: Immediate term, optimising current operations.

   - Horizon 2: Medium term, identifying new growth areas.

   - Horizon 3: Long term, exploring potential disruptions and innovations.

Continuous Learning and Personal Growth

1. **Reading widely:** Expands knowledge base and helps draw connections between diverse subjects.

2. **Networking:** Gaining new perspectives and insights from different sectors.

3. **Challenging assumptions:** Ensures not being limited by outdated beliefs, fostering innovation.

Big Data and Its Limitations

1. **Predicting future patterns:** Big data can reveal trends, predictive analytics and customer insights. However, it has limitations in fully predicting human behaviour due to humans' unpredictable nature.

2. **Cautionary tale – Nokia:** Despite using big data effectively, Nokia failed to anticipate the shift in consumer preferences towards smartphones with advanced features, leading to a dramatic decline in market share. This highlights the need to combine big data with qualitative insights and remain agile and innovative

Reflection Questions

1. How do you feel when you think about the future?

2. What makes an idea memorable?

ROLE MODELLING

Being a role model is the most powerful form of educating.

—John Wooden

The Power of Role Modelling

Role modelling is essential for managers who aim to lift others. It sets clear expectations of behaviour for team members. When managers practice what they preach, it creates a sense of *consistency*, which builds trust and credibility.

Role modelling can also help motivate team members as they strive to follow the exemplary behaviours of their managers. This can in turn influence team and even organisational dynamics as the glow of the team is noticed by others.

Managers who role model help to provide a live demonstration of desirable behaviours. They can help team members learn vital skills like problem-solving, decision-making and conflict resolution through modelling best practice.

Furthermore, role modelling can help to reinforce organisational culture. Managers can help imprint the values of the culture into daily operations by walking and talking these values. This can help bridge the disconnect staff often feel between the values and what happens on the ground. Most organisations espouse the values of the leadership route, but if managers don't embody these, it creates a general mistrust of the organisation and its culture. These become organisations with a toxic workplace culture and silent recognition that what is said and done are two very different things.

If managers role model Kelly (Theory X), then they will find their team members will appropriate these behaviours, believing that they are crucial for success. Team members will believe that competition and politics are key denominators for success, rather than transparency and collaboration. However, if they role model Sofia, they may well establish that collaboration and transparency are the keys to progress and promotion.

Role Modelling Sofia

Being a Sofia is challenging. However, by adopting certain behaviours we may be able to emulate her and, in turn, influence our team members and even our own managers. We can help to build a mini-culture within our own organisations: Sofia's Oasis. To role model Sofia, there are a few behaviours that we can adopt.

EMPOWERMENT THROUGH AUTONOMY

There's no greater way for a manager to communicate trust than through delegation. Managers can show this trust by delegating strategic elements of a project to team members. Of course, managers can only do this for team members who have the skill and motivation to do it, utilising the empowerment matrix. They should also avoid micromanaging as much as possible and frame directives as enabling rather than restricting conversations. Finally, managers can help team members feel a sense of autonomy in the way that they frame language. They can use inviting language 'is it ok if we have a chat?' rather than 'we need to have a chat', making it clear that people have some decision-making power in situations.

Encouraging Open Communication

Managers should build a culture of open communication. This means listening actively to team members and ensuring everyone has a voice. This might include making special efforts to listen to more introvert or reserved team members and ensuring that conversations are not dominated by the loudest people. Managers can also learn to give their opinions last so that they don't influence the conversations around their own goals too much. This can be challenging as managers might get excited or feel the need to assert control and spit out their opinions. Or they might telegraph their response to a decision simply through their body language.

Another behaviour managers should work on is giving people their attention in communication. This might mean stopping their work or looking up from their monitor to focus entirely on a team member. Managers who fail to do this are subconsciously communicating to their team that they lack importance.

Demonstrating Trust and Confidence

Managers can demonstrate trust in their team by sharing important information from higher up in the organisation. They can give them insights into higher-level discussions, which helps team members connect to the bigger picture and feel involved in something greater. Managers should also explicitly mention that they trust their team are capable of completing the work (or have the potential to). The affirmation, like the Pygmalion effect, can help build the confidence in team members, helping them to perform at higher levels.

Promoting Personal Development and Growth

I've lost count of the number of times where I have been delivering a training program and a participant has had to deal with the demands of their manager, nudging them in their inbox or phone or at worst, appearing in the training. Managers who support learning and personal growth ensure that their team have well-crafted learning journeys that match their interests *as well as* the time to focus on them.

Managers should be learners themselves and encourage others by role modelling the learning they are doing. This might involve sharing insights or recommending interesting learning material. Sofia also helps her team learn transferable skills to make them more agile at work. In addition, she models humility and doesn't claim to have all the answers or fall back on her expertise.

Importantly, Sofia models and rewards failure and vulnerability. She encourages team members to share mistakes and failure by talking about her own mistakes and shortcomings and connecting these failures to important lessons learned. This helps to inculcate a culture where failure is not seen as taboo but as a stepping stone to growth.

Exhibiting Empathy and Support

Sofia exhibits empathy and care for her team's professional and personal well-being. Managers can emulate this by being approachable and listening to their teams' concerns. They can work on asking questions when performance drops rather than simply jumping to conclusions. To get to a state of empathy, managers need to know their team and who they are. This means purposefully investing time in getting to know them and looking out for them. The more we know about someone, the more we can empathise with them.

Furthermore, managers should schedule regular check-ins to learn about and support team members through their challenges. There may be times where managers need to offer support or help team members adjust their work–life balance.

MODELLING RESILIENCE AND POSITIVITY

When times get rough, Sofia models resilience and positivity. By consistently bringing a positive energy, managers can influence the emotional state of others (sometimes referred to as emotional contagion).[1] When a manager consistently displays a positive attitude, it can help to create a more optimistic and resilient work environment. In contrast, if the manager is always pensive and low in energy, it can negatively impact the morale of the team.

Managers should also encourage their team to view challenges as opportunities for growth. This can help team members step outside their comfort zone into growth areas.

COLLABORATION AND TEAM SPIRIT

Sofia promotes a collaborative work environment where teamwork is actively encouraged. Managers can role model this by participating in team activities, facilitating collaboration amongst team members and recognising collective achievements. Managers should also organise team-building events or collaborative projects to help strengthen a sense of unity and community.

Role Modelling during High-stress Times

During stressful times, managers must be wary of resorting to more controlling behaviour. It is precisely during these times that managers must demonstrate trust, resilience and positive leadership. By maintaining a calm and constructive attitude, managers can help to prevent the spread of stress and anxiety in the team. This is precisely the time when managers need to express confidence in their team members' abilities, encourage collaboration and open communication.

Role modelling behaviours is a quick way for managers to start practising the behaviours of a leader who chooses the leadership route and lifts. If the manager was previously Theory X, it will take time for team members to adjust to the change. It may take the manager to actively tell team members that they are going to adjust their approach with the justification being organisational change or changing circumstances.

I've seen managers who have gone from Kelly to Sofia successfully. Some were simply unaware of a different way to manage and were overwhelmed by the possibilities of a new way of leading. Others, more sceptical, might find themselves saying that their context isn't suitable for such an approach or that their team weren't ready. My response would be, how much longer will Kelly prevail? We stand at a crossroads in leading and managing others.

Effective Managers Role-Model Checklist

Use the following as a checklist of effective behaviours to adopt if you want to take the leadership route and lead by lifting.

1. Empowerment Through Autonomy

Delegate project's strategic elements to team members, trusting them to set direction and make decisions.

Use inviting language rather than commanding, for example, 'Is it okay if we have a chat?' instead of 'We need to have a chat.'

Provide support and guidance when needed without micromanaging.

2. Encouraging Open Communication

Actively listen to team member's suggestions and concerns.

Hold regular team meetings where all voices are encouraged and heard.

Share your opinion last in discussions to truly listen to team input without influencing it too much.

Give undivided attention.

3. Demonstrating Trust and Confidence

Trust team members with important tasks, expressing confidence in their abilities.

Share important information from higher up in the organisation.

Explicitly share their trust in their team members' potential.

4. Promoting Personal and Professional Development

Encourage team members to attend workshops or pursue certifications.

Support professional development through training opportunities, mentorship and career planning.

Encourage the development of a range of transferable skills to keep the team agile and adaptable.

5. Exhibiting Empathy and Support

Be approachable and genuinely care about the well-being of your team, both professionally and personally.

Conduct one-on-one check-ins to understand and support employees' challenges.

Offer support or adjustments to help balance work and personal life.

6. Modelling Resilience and Positivity

Demonstrate a constructive attitude in the face of setbacks.

Encourage viewing challenges as opportunities for growth.

Exhibit a positive attitude, understanding the concept of emotional contagion to positively influence the team's emotional state.

7. Collaboration and Team Spirit

Actively participate in team activities and collaborative projects.

Facilitate collaboration between team members.

Recognise and celebrate collective achievements.

Organise team-building exercises to strengthen team cohesion and unity.

8. Role Modelling during High-Stress Times

Maintain a calm and constructive attitude under pressure.

Avoid reverting to controlling behaviours; demonstrate trust and resilience instead.

Exemplify confidence in team members' abilities, encouraging collaborative problem-solving.

Maintain open communication to prevent the spread of stress and anxiety.

Epilogue

Kelly

Kelly had always been a force to be reckoned with at Mango Bank. Her career, defined by a legacy of smashing targets, driving efficiency and hitting bottom-line goals, had helped the bank hit record profits, improve operations and improve its market share.

Now, sitting in her comfortable apartment in Singapore, surrounded by the spoils of her achievements, Kelly has plenty of time to reflect. Sometimes, as the shadows lengthen on the walls of her immaculate living room, doubts form in Kelly's mind, like the tiny termites that would chew her wooden bed frame back in her hometown, the thoughts would pick at her mind.

Had she really developed her people? That thought gnawed at her. Like a mother who worries whether her children are self-sufficient, Kelly would sometimes wonder if she had really developed her team. She prided herself on hitting targets, but growing talent? She had always believed in pushing her team to the limits. Now she wonders if that had been the right approach. Rupert had explained to her that it was precisely for that reason, he had given the MD role to someone else. The pain of that conversation is like a sharp thorn in her memories. Hadn't she developed others?!!

Kelly stares into space, pondering whether her team had followed her out of genuine respect or necessity. Some people had used the phrase 'tough but fair' to describe her but she suspects there might have been other more unpleasant accolades used. As the faces of some of the people she had upset float through her mind, she wonders how they might remember her, as a tyrant or as a trailblazer?

With a sigh, Kelly realises that she hadn't come out on top. What *really* is leadership, Kelly wonders. She had always believed it was about hitting targets. Now she doesn't feel so sure.

As Kelly pours herself a large glass of wine, she makes a silent toast to herself and Mango Bank. She lets her thoughts drift for a while, knowing that more doubts may resurface tomorrow. But tomorrow is another day she thinks, as she remembers her finely tuned timetable of activities.

Sofia

Sofia stands on top of the hill in Scotland, the wind pulling at her hair as she gazes at the heather-topped hills and fields surrounding her. The serene landscape is a long way from the frenetic energy of Mango Bank, but it somehow feels strangely familiar. Sofia had always savoured moments of quiet reflection, and this trip was providing her with some quiet time to look back.

Retirement had given Sofia the benefit of time, and she made sure she stayed in touch with her old team at Mango Bank. Their messages and updates proved to be a source of joy for her. The business was doing well and the practices which she had championed as MD were still in place. Her old team member Ganesh was now heading up the department and she was hearing great things about his leadership. Sofia smiles remembering a time when his performance at work had been underwhelming. She had seen the potential in him and her faith had paid off.

Sofia continued to hear stories of innovation. Her old team were not only excelling but they were transferring some of their best practice ideas to other units. The team had become a shining example of creativity and excellence within the organisation. As the wind ruffles her hair, Sofia realises this was a sign of the culture she had helped create.

As Sofia gazes out at the sheep in the fields below, she considers the essence of leadership. It wasn't about personal tributes or even hitting targets. Leadership was all about lifting others and helping them realise their potential. We aren't here forever, she muses. Legacy was really about the people we helped grow and the positive changes we instilled.

Sofia feels a surprising ache in her calf, a reminder of the Pilates class she has just started. Even in retirement, she was still enjoying new challenges and pushing herself.

Content and reflective, Sofia takes a deep breath and begins her descent down the hill. Her journey had taken her far, but for the next generation of leaders that journey was just beginning. It was a strangely comforting thought.

Self-Checkers Reference

This is the key for the self-checkers at the end of each chapter.

DISCLAIMER FOR SELF-CHECKERS

Please note that the self-checkers provided here, including the Effective Motivation Actions Checker for Managers, have not been scientifically validated or benchmarked for accuracy. They are intended as introspective tools to help you reflect on your management practices and identify potential areas for improvement. The results should be used as a guideline to stimulate thought and discussion rather than definitive assessments of your managerial abilities. It's recommended that these tools are used in conjunction with professional development resources or training to enhance your understanding and effectiveness in these areas.

For each statement below, rate how much you agree or disagree using the following scale:

- Strongly Disagree = 1 point

- Disagree = 2 points

- Neutral = 3 points

- Agree = 4 points

- Strongly Agree = 5 points

Calculate your total score after rating all the statements.

BELIEFS

Theory Y Indicator Statements: **1, 3, 5, 7, 9 (total of 25)** = _____

Minus

Theory X Indicator Statements: **2, 4, 6, 8, 10 (total of 25)** =_____

Your score: _____

Scoring:

Add up your score for Theory Y answers and minus the Theory X answer.

Score 16 to 20	You strongly believe in the potential and self-motivation of your team.
Score 10 to 15	You are starting with the right mindset to adopt the ideas in this book.
Score 5 to 9	You have a good understanding of Theory Y principles but may have some areas to develop further.
Score 0 to 4	You are inclined towards Theory Y, but with some hesitation.
Score −1 to −4	You tend to believe more in the principles of Theory X, with some inclination towards control and supervision.
Score −5 to −9	You believe in the need for active management intervention and control to get work done.
Score −10 to −15	You have a strong belief in the necessity of close supervision and control over your team.
Score −16 to −20	You strongly believe that most people dislike work and require strict supervision and control.

MINDSET

Growth Mindset Indicators Statements: **1, 3, 5, 7, 9 (total of 25)** = _____

Minus

Fixed Mindset Indicators Statements: **2, 4, 6, 8, 10 (total of 25)** = _____

Your Score: _____

Add up your score for Growth Mindset answers and minus the Fixed Mindset answers.

Score 16 to 20	You strongly believe in the potential for growth and development through effort and perseverance.
Score 10 to 15	You are starting with the right mindset to adopt the ideas in this book.
Score 5 to 9	You have a good understanding of growth mindset principles but may have some areas to develop further.
Score 0 to 4	You are inclined towards a growth mindset, but with some hesitation.
Score −1 to −4	You tend to believe more in fixed traits, with some inclination towards a fixed mindset.
Score −5 to −9	You believe in the necessity of innate talent and fixed intelligence.
Score −10 to −15	You have a strong belief in the immutability of intelligence and talent.
Score −16 to −20	You strongly believe that abilities are fixed and cannot be significantly developed through effort.

DIRECTING

Effective Direction Statements: **1, 3, 5, 7, 9 (total of 25)** = _____

Minus

Ineffective Direction Actions Statements: **2, 4, 6, 8, 10 (total of 25)** = _____

Your Score: _____

Add up your score for Effective Direction answers and minus the Ineffective Direction answers.

Score 16 to 20	You excel in providing clear and supportive direction to your team.
Score 10 to 15	You are starting with the right mindset to adopt effective direction strategies.
Score 5 to 9	You have a good understanding of effective direction principles but may have some areas to develop further.
Score 0 to 4	You are inclined towards effective direction, but with some hesitation.
Score −1 to −4	You tend to lean more towards ineffective direction practices, with some inclination towards quick instructions and minimal support.
Score −5 to −9	You believe in quick instructions and minimal support, often assuming that minimal guidance is sufficient.
Score −10 to −15	You strongly believe in minimal direction and expect immediate understanding and perfection from your team.
Score −16 to −20	You strongly believe that abilities are fixed and cannot be significantly developed through effort.

DELEGATING

Effective Delegation Actions Statements: **1, 3, 5, 7, 9, 11 (total of 30)** = _____

Minus

Ineffective Delegation Actions Statements: **2, 4, 6, 8, 10, 12 (total of 30)**

= _____

Your Score: _____

Add up your score for Effective Delegation answers and minus the Ineffective Delegation answers.

Score 18 to 24	You excel in delegation, providing clear goals, resources and support to your team, fostering trust and understanding.
Score 12 to 17	You have a strong approach to delegation, often setting clear expectations and offering support, though there may be occasional gaps.
Score 6 to 11	You understand the principles of effective delegation but may lack consistency in providing support or clear direction.
Score 0 to 5	You tend to be somewhat effective in delegation but may not always provide the necessary resources, support or clarity, and your actions may be inconsistent.
Score −1 to −6	You lean towards ineffective delegation, often assuming tasks will be handled independently without providing sufficient support or clarity.
Score −7 to −12	You tend to delegate without adequate support, resources or follow-up, assuming minimal guidance is enough.
Score −13 to −18	You believe in minimal direction and often delegate without considering the team member's capabilities or providing necessary resources.
Score −19 to −24	You strongly believe that minimal direction is sufficient and often fail to offer the support or clarity needed for effective task completion.

MOTIVATING

Effective Motivation Actions Statements: **1, 3, 5, 7, 9, 11 (total of 30)** = _____

Minus

Ineffective Motivation Actions Statements: **2, 4, 6, 8, 10, 12 (total of 30)** = _____

Your Score: _____

Add up your score for Effective Motivation answers and minus the Ineffective Motivation answers.

Score 18 to 24	You excel in motivating your team, consistently recognising effort, providing meaningful feedback and involving them in goal-setting.
Score 12 to 17	You have a strong approach to motivation, often praising effort and offering support, though there may be occasional gaps.
Score 6 to 11	You understand the principles of effective motivation but may lack consistency in offering feedback or involving your team in their development.
Score 0 to 5	You tend to be somewhat effective in motivation but may not always provide the necessary recognition, feedback or support, leading to inconsistency.
Score −1 to −6	You lean towards ineffective motivation, often overlooking the importance of effort-based recognition and specific feedback.
Score −7 to −12	You tend to provide vague feedback and may not engage your team in goal-setting or support them adequately in their development.
Score −13 to −18	You believe in minimal involvement in your team's motivation, often expecting them to drive their development without much support.
Score −19 to −24	You strongly believe that motivation is solely intrinsic and rarely provide the feedback, recognition or support needed to help your team grow.

DIFFICULT CONVERSATIONS

Effective Difficult Conversation Actions Statements: **1, 3, 5, 7, 9, 10 (total of 30) =** _____

Minus

Ineffective Difficult Conversation Actions Statements: **2, 4, 6, 8, 11, 12 (total of 30) =** _____

Your Score _____

Add up your score for Effective Difficult Conversation answers and minus the Ineffective Difficult Conversation answers.

Score 18 to 24	You excel in handling difficult conversations, addressing issues promptly, providing specific feedback and working with employees to find constructive solutions.
Score 12 to 17	You have a strong approach to difficult conversations, often addressing issues with empathy and respect, though there may be occasional gaps in how you provide feedback or involve the employee.
Score 6 to 11	You understand the principles of effective difficult conversations but may lack consistency in offering specific examples or involving the employee in developing improvement plans.
Score 0 to 5	You tend to be somewhat effective in handling difficult conversations, but may not always provide the necessary examples, support or constructive focus, leading to inconsistency.

Score —1 to —6	You lean towards ineffective difficult conversations, often avoiding difficult discussions, providing vague feedback or lacking empathy and respect.
Score —7 to —12	You tend to focus on the negatives without providing specific examples or constructive solutions, often dominating the conversation and leaving the employee to figure out improvements on their own.
Score —13 to —18	You believe in minimal involvement during difficult conversations, often focusing on blame rather than solutions, and rarely involving the employee in finding ways to improve.
Score —19 to —24	You strongly believe that difficult conversations should be one-sided, focusing only on the negatives without offering support or constructive feedback.

COACHING

Effective Non-Directive Coaching Actions: Statements **1, 3, 5, 7, 9 (total of 25)** =

_____

Minus

Ineffective Directive Coaching Actions: Statements **2, 4, 6, 8, 10 (total of 25)** =

_____

Your Score _____

Add up your score for Effective Non-Directive Coaching Actions answers and minus the Ineffective Directive Coaching actions.

Score 16 to 20	You excel in coaching, consistently encouraging self-reflection, active listening and empowering employees to find their own solutions.
Score 10 to 15	You have a strong approach to coaching, often providing a balance between guidance and allowing the employee to explore their own solutions, though there may be occasional gaps.
Score 5 to 9	You understand the principles of effective coaching but may lack consistency in fostering self-reflection or encouraging employee-driven goal-setting.
Score 0 to 4	You tend to be somewhat effective in coaching, but may not always provide the necessary space for the employee to reflect or take ownership of their development, leading to inconsistency.

Score —1 to —4	You lean towards ineffective coaching, often focusing more on giving direct advice and sharing your own experiences rather than encouraging the employee to find their own solutions.
Score —5 to —9	You tend to take control of coaching conversations, providing advice and solutions rather than fostering an environment where the employee can reflect and set their own goals.
Score —10 to —15	You believe in a directive approach to coaching, often telling rather than asking, and relying heavily on your own expertise to solve the employee's issues.
Score —16 to —20	You strongly believe in a top-down approach to coaching, rarely allowing the employee to contribute their thoughts, and primarily focusing on your own solutions and experiences.

INFLUENCE

Effective Influence-Based Leadership Actions: Statements **1, 3, 5, 7, 9**

(total of 25) = _____

Ineffective Influence-Based Leadership Actions: Statements **2, 4, 6, 8, 10**

(total of 25) = _____

Your Score _____

Add up your score for Effective Influence answers and minus the Ineffective Influence answers.

Score 16 to 20	You excel in influence-based leadership, consistently building rapport, seeking input and leading by example, while minimising reliance on formal authority.
Score 10 to 15	You have a strong approach to influence-based leadership, often engaging your team and leading by example, though there may be occasional reliance on authority.
Score 5 to 9	You understand the principles of influence-based leadership but may lack consistency in fostering collaboration and trust without resorting to formal power.
Score 0 to 4	You tend to be somewhat effective in influence-based leadership but may not always avoid the use of authority or position to enforce decisions, leading to inconsistency.
Score —1 to —4	You lean towards ineffective influence-based leadership, often relying on your formal position to assert control rather than building trust and collaboration.
Score —5 to —9	You tend to dominate discussions and use your position to enforce decisions, focusing less on influence and more on authority.

Score —10 to —15	You believe in a directive approach to leadership, often reminding your team of your position and using authority to get things done.
Score —16 to —20	You strongly rely on formal power and position to lead, rarely engaging in influence-based practices like collaboration, trust-building or leading by example.

Thinking BIG

Big Picture Thinker Statements: **2, 3, 4, 7, 13, 14, 15, 17, 19, 20 (total of 50)**

= _____

Minus

Detail Focus Statements: **1, 5, 6, 8, 9, 10, 11, 12, 16, 18 (total of 50)** = _____

Your Score _____

Add up your score for Big Picture Thinker answers and minus the Detail Focus answers.

Score 30 to 40	You are a visionary thinker, constantly exploring new ideas, seeing patterns and focusing on the bigger picture. You thrive in dynamic environments and are driven by the possibilities of the future.
Score 20 to 29	You have a strong inclination towards big-picture thinking, often engaging in creative brainstorming and future-oriented planning, though you may occasionally get caught up in details.
Score 10 to 19	You understand and appreciate big-picture thinking but may balance it with a need for routine and familiarity. You're capable of seeing the broader vision but may some-times focus on process and details.
Score 0 to 9	You show a moderate level of big-picture thinking, but often rely on routine tasks and familiar processes. You can think creatively but may prefer structure and order in your work.

Score —1 to —9	You lean towards detail-oriented thinking, often focusing on routine and process rather than exploring new ideas or thinking creatively. You may struggle with seeing the bigger picture.
Score —10 to —19	You prefer structured, linear work and are often sceptical of change and new ideas. Big-picture thinking may feel overwhelming or impractical to you.
Score —20 to —29	You rely heavily on routine and are cautious about change. You find comfort in familiar tasks and processes and may resist creative thinking or brainstorming sessions.
Score —30 to —40	You strongly favour routine, detail-oriented work and are often suspicious of new ideas. You are highly focused on processes and may struggle to see the broader vision or future possibilities.

Notes

Chapter 1

1. Taylor, F.W. (1911). *The Principles of Scientific Management*. New York: Harper & Brothers.

2. McGregor, D. (1960). *The Human Side of Enterprise*. New York: McGraw-Hill.

3. Ouchi, W.G. (1981). *Theory Z: How American Business Can Meet the Japanese Challenge*. Reading, MA: Addison-Wesley.

4. Rosenthal, R. and Jacobson, L. (1968). *Pygmalion in the Classroom: Teacher Expectation and Pupils' Intellectual Development*. New York: Holt, Rinehart & Winston.

5. Eden, D. (1990). *Pygmalion in Management: Productivity as a Self-Fulfilling Prophecy*. Lexington Books.

6. Maslow, A.H. (1943). A theory of human motivation. *Psychological Review*, 50 (4), 370–396.

7. Herzberg, F., Mausner, B., and Snyderman, B.B. (1959). *The Motivation to Work*. New York: Wiley.

8. Klotz, A.C. and Bolino, M.C. (2018). *Do You Have a 'Calling'? An Examination of People Who Are Willing to Sacrifice Pay to Do Meaningful Work*. Harvard Business Review.

9. Malone, T.W. (2004). *The Future of Work: How the New Order of Business Will Shape Your Organization, Your Management Style, and Your Life*. Harvard Business School Press.

10. Deloitte (2023). *Gen Z and Millennial Survey 2023*. Deloitte.

Chapter 2

1. Edmondson, A.C. (2018). *The Fearless Organization: Creating Psychological Safety in the Workplace for Learning, Innovation, and Growth.* Wiley.

2. Duhigg, C. (2016). What Google learned from its quest to build the perfect team. *The New York Times Magazine* (25 February).

3. Rock, D. (2008). SCARF: a brain-based model for collaborating with and influencing others. *NeuroLeadership Journal* 1 (1): 1–9.

4. Dweck, C.S. (2006). *Mindset: The New Psychology of Success.* Random House.

5. Gilbert, D. (2006). *Stumbling on Happiness.* Knopf.

6. Baldwin, N. (2001). *Edison: Inventing the Century.* University of Chicago Press.

7. Clark, D. (2016). *Alibaba: The House That Jack Ma Built.* HarperCollins.

8. Morita, A., Reingold, E.M., and Shimomura, M. (1986). *Made in Japan: Akio Morita and Sony.* Dutton.

9 Wallace, A. (1986). *The Prodigy: A Biography of William James Sidis, America's Greatest Child Prodigy.* Macmillan Publishing Company.

Chapter 3

1. Hersey, P. and Blanchard, K.H. (1969). *Management of Organizational Behavior: Utilizing Human Resources.* Prentice Hall.

Chapter 4

1. Seki, K. (1963). *Urashima Taro and Other Japanese Children's Stories*. Tokyo: Tuttle Publishing.

2. Burch, N. (1970). *The Four Stages for Learning Any New Skill*. Gordon Training International.

3. Kahneman, D. (2011). *Thinking, Fast and Slow*. Farrar, Straus and Giroux.

4. Bloom, B.S. (1956). *Taxonomy of Educational Objectives: The Classification of Educational Goals, Handbook I: Cognitive Domain*. Longman.

Chapter 5

1. American Management Association (2023). *Survey on delegation and task management*. American Management Association. https://www.amanet.org (American Management Association).

2. Gallup (2017). *State of the American Workplace*. Gallup, Inc.

3. Institute for Corporate Productivity (i4cp) (2007). *You Want It When?* i4cp. Retrieved from https://www.i4cp.com

4. Arootah (2023). 3 Fears that keep leaders from delegating (and how to overcome them). https://arootah.com/blog/business-and-leadership/leadership-and-management/how-to-overcome-delegation-fears/ (accessed 13 November 2024).

Chapter 6

1. Gallup (2019). *The Importance of Weekly Feedback*. Gallup.

2. Mueller, C.M. and Dweck, C.S. (1998). Praise for intelligence can undermine children's motivation and performance. *Journal of Personality and Social Psychology* 75 (1): 33–52.

3. Csikszentmihalyi, M. (1990). *Flow: The Psychology of Optimal Experience*. Harper & Row.

4. Goldsmith, M. (2002). Try feedforward instead of feedback. *Leader to Leader* 25: 11-13.

Chapter 7

1. Alberti, R.E. and Emmons, M.L. (2008). *Your Perfect Right: Assertiveness and Equality in Your Life and Relationships* , 9e. Impact Publishers.

2. Hofstede, G. (1980). *Culture's Consequences: International Differences in Work-Related Values.* Sage Publications

3. Chen, G.M. and Starosta, W.J. (2005). *Foundations of Intercultural Communication*. University Press of America.

4. Stoate, A. (2018). A Leader's Guide to Difficult Conversations. LinkedIn (9 May). https://www.linkedin.com/pulse/leaders-guide-todifficult-conversations-aidan-stoate (accessed 18 October 2024).

Chapter 8

1. International Coaching Federation (n.d.). What is coaching? https://coachingfederation.org/about (accessed 13 November 2024).

2. Krishnamurti, J. (1995). *The Book of Life: Daily Meditations with Krishnamurti.* HarperOne.

3. Goman, C.K. (2008). *The Nonverbal Advantage: Secrets and Science of Body Language at Work.* Berrett-Koehler Publishers.

4. O'Connor, J. and Seymour, J. (1995). *Introducing NLP: Psychological Skills for Understanding and Influencing People.* Thorsons.

5. Whitmore, J. (2009). *Coaching for Performance: Growing Human Potential and Purpose – The Principles and Practice of Coaching and Leadership* 4. Nicholas Brealey Publishing.

Chapter 9

1. Twenge, J.M. and Campbell, S.M. (2008). Generational differences in psychological traits and their impact on the workplace. *Journal of Managerial Psychology* 23 (8): 862–877.

2. Baker, T. (2015). *The New Influencing Toolkit: Capabilities for Communicating with Influence.* Palgrave Macmillan.

3. Northouse, P.G. (2018). *Leadership: Theory and Practice.* SAGE Publications.

4. Kahneman, D. (2011). Thinking, Fast and Slow. *Farrar, Straus, and Giroux.*

5. Damasio, A.R. (1994). *Descartes' Error: Emotion, Reason, and the Human Brain.* G.P. Putnam's Sons.

6. Dolan, G. (2017). *Stories for Work: The Essential Guide to Business Storytelling.* Wiley.

7. Zak, P.J. (2015). Why inspiring stories make us react: the neuroscience of narrative. *Cerebrum* (2 February): 2.

8 Zak, P.J. (2012). *The Moral Molecule: How Trust Works.* Dutton.

Chapter 10

1. Baghai, M., Coley, S., and White, D. (1999). *The Alchemy of Growth: Practical Insights for Building the Enduring Enterprise (McKinsey & Company).* Perseus Books Group.

2. Cooper, A., Reimann, R., Cronin, D., et al. (2014). *About Face: The Essentials of Interaction Design* (4). Wiley.

3. Smith, S.M. and Blankenship, S.E. (1991). Incubation and the persistence of fixation in problem solving. *American Journal of Psychology* 104 (1): 61–87.

4. Stickgold, R. (2005). Sleep-dependent memory consolidation. *Nature* 437 (7063): 1272–1278.

Chapter 11

1. Barsade, S.G. (2002). The ripple effect: emotional contagion and its influence on group behavior. *Administrative Science Quarterly* 47 (4): 644–675.